FREDERICK THE GREAT

and

The Rise of Prussia

is one of the volumes
in the
TEACH YOURSELF HISTORY
LIBRARY

Teach Yourself History

FREDERICK THE GREAT

and

The Rise of Prussia

by

D. B. HORN

Professor of Modern History
in the University of Edinburgh

THE ENGLISH UNIVERSITIES PRESS LTD
102 Newgate Street
LONDON E.C.1

FIRST PRINTED 1964

Copyright © 1964
D. B. Horn

PRINTED AND BOUND IN ENGLAND FOR
THE ENGLISH UNIVERSITIES PRESS LTD., BY
HAZELL WATSON AND VINEY LTD, AYLESBURY, BUCKS

A General Introduction to the Series

THIS series has been undertaken in the conviction that there can be no subject of study
more important than history. Great as have been
the conquests of natural science in our time—such
that many think of ours as a scientific age *par
excellence*—it is even more urgent and necessary
that advances should be made in the social
sciences, if we are to gain control of the forces of
nature loosed upon us. The bed out of which all
the social sciences spring is history; there they find,
in greater or lesser degree, subject-matter and
material, verification or contradiction.

There is no end to what we can learn from
history, if only we would, for it is conterminous with
life. Its special field is the life of man in society,
and at every point we can learn vicariously from
the experience of others before us in history.

To take one point only—the understanding of
politics: how can we hope to understand the world
of affairs around us if we do not know how it came
to be what it is? How to understand Germany or
Soviet Russia, or the United States—or ourselves,
without knowing something of their history?

There is no subject that is more useful, or indeed indispensable.

Some evidence of the growing awareness of this may be seen in the immense increase in the interest of the reading public in history, and the much larger place the subject has come to take in education in our time.

This series has been planned to meet the needs and demands of a very wide public and of education—they are indeed the same. I am convinced that the most congenial, as well as the most concrete and practical, approach to history is the biographical, through the lives of the great men whose actions have been so much part of history, and whose careers in turn have been so moulded and formed by events.

The key idea of this series, and what distinguishes it from any other that has appeared, is the intention by way of a biography of a great man to open up a significant historical theme; for example, Cromwell and the Puritan Revolution, or Lenin and the Russian Revolution.

My hope is, in the end, as the series fills out and completes itself, by a sufficient number of biographies to cover whole periods and subjects in that way. To give you the history of the United States, for example, or the British Empire or France, *via* a number of biographies of their leading historical figures.

That should be something new, as well as convenient and practical, in education.

I need hardly say that I am a strong believer in people with good academic standards writing once more for the general reading public, and of the public being given the best that the universities can provide. From this point of view this series is intended to bring the university into the homes of the people.

A. L. ROWSE

ALL SOULS COLLEGE,
    OXFORD.

Contents

Maps

Preface

THIS book begins with a brief discussion of the contributions made by Frederick the Great's predecessors to the rise of Prussia and reviews the stormy story of his relationship to his father, Frederick William I. It then seeks to explain how Prussia under Frederick the Great came to be generally recognized as the equal of Austria and a great power. Dualism was effectively established in the Holy Roman Empire and remained the keynote of German politics for over a century until Bismarck expelled Austria in 1866 and forced the other German states into the Hohenzollern Empire in 1871. Military strength and an efficient bureaucracy, both despotically controlled by the Prussian king through the 'cabinet' system of government, and supported by mercantilist control of economic resources and the social predominance of the Junker class, created a state that was unique in Europe. The Prussian system of government denied the middle and lower classes any chance of political education, and prevented the development of responsible government. When Prussia, led by Bismarck, captured Germany, this had fatal consequences, both internally and externally. Bismarck was Frederick's true heir and successor, though the Frederician myth contributed almost as much to the making of the Third (or Nazi) Reich in the twentieth century as it had to the erection of the Hohenzollern Empire in the nineteenth.

D. B. HORN

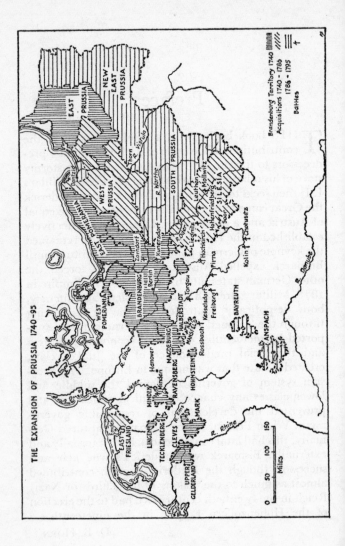

THE EXPANSION OF PRUSSIA 1740–95

Brandenburg Territory 1740
Acquisitions 1740 – 1786
           1786 – 1795
Battles

EAST PRUSSIA

NEW EAST PRUSSIA

WEST PRUSSIA

EAST POMERANIA

WEST POMERANIA

SOUTH PRUSSIA

BRANDENBURG

Berlin

Danzig

R. Vistula

Thorn

R. Warthe

SILESIA

Zorndorf

Kunersdorf

R. Oder

Liegnitz

Leuthen

Mollwitz

Hohenfriedberg

Hochkirch

Pirna

Kolin

Chotusitz

Soor

Freiberg

Kesselsdorf

Torgau

Rossbach

MAGDEBURG

HALBERSTADT

MINDEN

Hanover

MÜNSTER

RAVENSBERG

HOHNSTEIN

BAYREUTH

ANSPACH

R. Danube

MARK

CLEVES

UPPER GELDERLAND

R. Rhine

R. Ems

TECKLENBERG

LINGEN

EAST FRIESLAND

R. Weser

R. Elbe

0   50   100   150
Miles

Chapter One

Brandenburg-Prussia before 1740

THE rise and fall of empires is one of the few constants in history and has attracted attention from classical times to the present day. Historians of modern Europe have made generalizations about the pre-eminence in each century of one Great Power. Sometimes this is no more than military and political ascendancy: at other times military and political ascendancy has contributed to and sometimes been promoted by a massive contribution of the politically dominant power to European civilization.

When a new Great Power has appeared in modern Europe it is rarely possible to date its emergence precisely. Thus, to take the case of Russia, historians differ over the claims of Peter I and Catherine II to be the ruler under whom Russia achieved Great Power status. While it is impossible to question the importance of Russia's rôle in eastern Europe under Peter the Great and his successors, it is not until the reign of Catherine II that western Europe came to look on Russia as a great European power. This particular difficulty hardly exists in the case of Prussia which, owing to its geographical situation, political interests and diplomatic traditions, had a foot both in the east and in the west European camps. Most, though by no means all, Prussian historians have assumed rather than argued that the rise of Prussia was the life-work of Frederick the Great.

Admittedly he could not have done what he did but for the achievements of his predecessors. Frederick William, the Great Elector (1640–88), not only gained valuable provinces, but began the process of subjecting all his territories, old and new, to an efficient and remarkably centralized bureaucracy. He built up an army which at Fehrbellin in 1675 proved itself capable of defeating the Swedes, then the leading military power in Europe. He introduced the excise and developed the economy with the help of industrious Huguenot refugees from France. His alliance with France, though not a success at the time, pointed the way to Frederick II's foreign policy in the early years of his reign.

The Great Elector's son, Frederick, showed less interest in politics and war. He founded the University of Halle, started the Prussian Academy at Berlin and built palaces closely modelled on Versailles. More important, however, was his one political success. As a reward for helping Austria against the French in the war of the Spanish succession, he secured from a reluctant Emperor the title of King, not of Brandenburg where he continued to rule, as his ancestors had done for centuries, as Elector, but of East Prussia, which was not included in the Holy Roman Empire and since 1660 had been ruled as a sovereign duchy by the electors of Brandenburg.

The achievement of royal *status* was a solid asset to the house of Brandenburg, although its importance was somewhat diminished because the Hohenzollerns' north German rivals, the rulers of Saxony and Hanover, also became kings, respectively, of Poland and Great Britain. On the other hand to qualify for kingship as Augustus I in Poland the Elector Augustus II of Saxony became a convert to Roman Catholicism. He thus forfeited the acknowledged leadership of German Protestantism which his predecessors had held since the Reformation. In the eighteenth century Brandenburg and Hanover gradually succeeded in taking over from Saxony the leadership of the German Protestants and as a rule combined to resist Hapsburg proselytism and persecution in central Europe. And too late the Saxon kings of Poland realized that the Polish crown was a source of weakness rather than of strength to their dynasty. They failed to gain effective control of their kingdom, while the resources of Saxony proved an inadequate basis for the extended political views which their new acquisition forced them to adopt.

When in 1714 the electors of Hanover acquired

the title of king of Great Britain this undoubtedly raised their prestige in the Empire and intensified their rivalry with Brandenburg. But here too it soon became manifest that the Hanoverian kings, although they could exert influence on British foreign policy, could not hope to gain personal control of the resources of their new kingdom. Both George I and George II looked on their English subjects as king-killers and republicans and in the main respected the restrictions imposed on them by the growing constitutional conventions of their island kingdom. Indeed the acquisition of a royal title endangered Hanover as much as it did Saxony, because Hanover now became involved, through its British connexion, with all the diplomatic crises and wars of the eighteenth century. In spite of electoral attempts to negotiate treaties of neutrality for Hanover, the unfortunate electorate became a battlefield upon which Britain and France fought out their colonial rivalry. Even if Britain won, the most that Hanover could hope for was its restoration to the position it had occupied before the war.

Thus of the three leading north German powers of the beginning of the eighteenth century, Brandenburg alone really profited from the acquisition of a royal title. The King ruled as absolutely in Prussia as the Elector had done and Brandenburg did not become involved in any new diplomatic or military responsibilities. The

Hohenzollerns had been admitted to the coveted position of crowned heads of states with its attendant *mystique* and practical consequences. Admission to this rank was a tangible recognition of the advances made by Brandenburg in the second half of the seventeenth century and automatically stimulated the ambitions of Frederick I's successors.

His son, Frederick William I was a ruler of another type, almost completely destitute of his father's interest in scholarship, literature and the arts, though he found in the practice of painting some relief from the physical pain and mental obsessions which haunted his later years. He concentrated fiercely on establishing royal despotism throughout his scattered dominions. Taken up with the problems of power, he devoted his life to creating an army and a centralized bureaucracy, whose primary function was to raise taxation to pay for his army.

By 1740 the Prussian army of 83,000 men was the fourth largest in Europe, although, when the states of Europe are arranged in order of population at this time, Prussia was only thirteenth. To keep his army up to strength, Frederick William conscripted his own subjects and kidnapped those of his neighbours; but, by associating each regiment with a specific territory or canton within his dominions, he ensured that it would remain a national force. Officers were recruited mainly from the Prussian nobility who were the natural leaders of an army of conscripted peasants. Unending parade ground drill, supplemented by reviews and field exercises, forged a weapon without which Frederick the Great could have achieved little.

It was Frederick William I who broke down the distinction, dating from the reign of the Great Elector, between civil and military institutions. The General War Commissariat, which had gradually extended its authority from military taxation to the collection of excise duties and the control of municipal government, was merged in 1723 with the General Finance Directory, which had come to be responsible for civil taxation, the collection of revenue from the royal domains and the management of the postal services.

The competition between these two rival organizations with no clear-cut division of function was intensified because both were also competing with older agencies responsible in some provinces to the local estates and not to the Elector. From 1723 a single organization, the General Directory, collected all taxation and other crown revenues and supervised all the activities of the provincial authorities. Not only were peculiar Prussian institutions developed to serve the needs of the army. These exerted almost as much influence on economic development and social life. Everything was subordinated to keeping up the military establishment and increasing the number and effectiveness of the armed forces.

Partly for this reason, Frederick William I modified the use of the cabinet council under his presidency, which dated back to the Great Elector's time and had taken over much of the work of government formerly discharged by an increasingly fossilized Privy Council. This process had been in harmony with the constitutional development of most of the more important German states; but by 1723 Frederick William I had set up a system of cabinet government peculiar to Prussia. Under this system decisions were reserved to the king himself who worked in his 'cabinet' and communicated his orders to his ministers by letters written by one or other of his personal secretaries.

Another feature of Frederick William's bureaucracy was his adoption of the system by which administrative business was assigned to 'colleges', each specializing in a particular kind of business, e.g. foreign affairs. Each college had several officials, some senior and some junior, but no single head. The General Directory for instance had five directors of equal rank, each responsible for all its decisions, and fourteen subordinate officers who were responsible only for the work done in their own departments. One main object of the collegiate system of administration, which was by no means peculiar to Prussia, was to prevent too much power falling into the hands of any one administrator. For the same reason Frederick William I showed distrust of the nobles as administrators and preferred to rely upon middle class civil servants and lawyers who had no local influence and owed their positions entirely to the crown.

Frederick William I had certainly made Brandenburg-Prussia a state capable of greatness, but the history of his reign and especially of his foreign policy shows that as long as he reigned the potentialities of the new kingdom could never be realized.

Chapter Two

The Youth of Frederick the Great 1712–30

FREDERICK was born at Berlin on 24 January 1712. He was the third son of Frederick William I of Brandenburg-Prussia, but his two elder brothers had both died before he was born. His mother was Sophia Dorothea, sister of George the Elector of Hanover who, two years later, became also George I, King of Great Britain. Although he had thirteen brothers and sisters only one, Wilhelmina, his elder by three years, meant much to him and only Henry (born in 1726) played any part in the politics of his reign. The name Frederick was bestowed upon him by his grandfather, the first king of Prussia, in the belief that this name had always brought luck to the Hohenzollerns.

His father, who succeeded to the throne in 1713, at first entrusted the education of his children to the French Huguenot refugee who had been his own governess, Madame de Rocoulle, and to the son of another Huguenot, Duhan de Jandun, who had caught Frederick William's eye by his bravery at the siege of Stralsund. Frederick's native language soon came to be, and remained all his life, French. On his own showing he spoke German like a coachman. Certainly he hardly ever used German in his correspondence, except when sending orders to illiterate army officers or provincial officials. When the infant prince reached boyhood, his father added to his tutors General Finck von Finckenstein, a veteran soldier of sixty, and Colonel Kalkstein, who had distinguished himself at Malplaquet.

About this time Frederick William prescribed in elaborate detail the way in which his son should spend every hour of every day of every week. Rising promptly at 6 on weekdays and at 7 on Sundays the boy was to put on his slippers, pray aloud at his bedside, wash himself, comb his hair, and drink a cup of tea or coffee for breakfast. Family prayers, lessons, lectures from his tutor on religion and morality and regular outdoor exercise fill up the week during the hours when the boy's attendance upon his father was not required. If he passed a weekly examination he was to be allowed Saturday afternoon to himself and in any case after mid-day dinner on Sunday 'the rest of the day is his own'.

Frederick William expressly forbade the study of Latin. Modern history was to be studied carefully, ancient history very superficially, if at all. Mathematics and especially the science of fortification were essential. Political economy and international law were to take the time usually occupied by Latin. Most important of all Fritz was to be taught to regard his father as his best friend. Therefore the tutors might use threats to make him afraid of his mother, but never of his father. Even before this Fritz's military education had begun when his father organized a company of boy soldiers with whom the six-year-old Crown Prince was regularly drilled. Later his father presented him with a model arsenal, fitted up with every conceivable weapon of war.

Since Frederick, even in his teens, was not likely to submit for long to such regimentation without a struggle, conflict between father and son was no doubt inevitable. Moreover in eighteenth-century royal houses conflict between the reigning sovereign and his hereditary successor was, as it were, built in. Opponents of the sovereign and other malcontents naturally gravitated towards his successor in the hope of indoctrinating him or at least securing some kind of protection. The sovereign came to see in his son's accession a threat to all that he had achieved in his own lifetime, suspected him of looking forward with pleasurable anticipation to his father's death and mentally charged him with high treason towards the state.

At Frederick William's court a ding-dong battle was being waged between the English party headed by Queen Sophia Dorothea, and the

Austrian party headed by Seckendorff, an old companion in arms of the king, now in the Austrian service but frequently resident at Berlin, and Frederick William's minister, Grumbkow, who was also the paid agent of the court of Vienna. Frederick William in his own odd way was still fond of Sophia Dorothea and allowed her a palace of her own at Monbijou. There she entertained foreign envoys and tried to impress them with the sophistication and culture which—notoriously absent at her husband's court—was already traditional at Hanover. But he had nothing but contempt for his Hanoverian relations and was determined to remain sole master of Prussian policy. This was formulated mainly in the celebrated tobacco college when, after a long day in the hunting field, the king and his cronies, headed by Grumbkow and Seckendorff and including his favourite generals, met to smoke their post-prandial pipes uninhibited by female society.

The first overt breach between Frederick and his father seems to have occurred at a dinner party given by Grumbkow in 1724 when the king told the company that he knew Frederick did not think as he did and asserted that some people were trying to instil quite contrary ideas into his son's head. He then publicly admonished his son to keep a good army and plenty of money since in these two things lay the glory and security of a king. While he was speaking he emphasized what he was saying by tapping his son, gently at first, on the cheeks and finished by boxing his ears. He did not explain who the scoundrels were who were alienating his son's affections and making him think differently from his father, but presumably they included Sophia Dorothea and the crown princess Wilhelmina. Consequently the quarrel between Frederick and his father, which continued until Frederick William's death sixteen years later, if not longer, combined the worst features of personal incompatibility, family feud and political controversy.

Even judged by contemporary standards, the king's treatment of his son and heir can only be described as pathological. He made a scene if the boy wore gloves while out hunting when it was hard frost and beat him for using a three pronged silver fork instead of a two pronged steel one. He fondled his younger son Augustus Wilhelm (born 1722) and publicly contrasted his good qualities with the depraved character of his elder brother. Frederick would have been less than human had he not determined at this early stage to get even with his father. And he was clearly being egged on by Wilhelmina, if not also by his mother. We might be disposed to reject some of the details of the horrible family feud as related by Wilhelmina, who certainly had a talent for dramatizing the events of her home life which would have earned her rich rewards from the twentieth-century popular press. But the essential features of the story are confirmed by the dispatches of contemporary diplomatists at the Prussian Court who had access to diverse and independent sources of information.

In the international crisis caused by violent Franco–British reaction to the alliance of Austria and Spain in 1725, Frederick William first joined with France and Britain and made proposals for a double marriage between the royal houses of Hohenzollern and Hanover. Wilhelmina was to Harry Frederick, Duke of Gloucester, the Prince of Wales's elder son, while Frederick of Hohenzollern would take as his bride one of the daughters of the Prince of Wales, probably the princess Amelia. Since the double marriage would have linked Prussia irrevocably with England, it became a principal object of Austrian policy to prevent it taking place. Seckendorff was sent to live at the Prussian court in 1726 and thanks to his personal influence over the king, combined with his skilful bribery of Frederick William's confidants and servants, Prussia left the league of Hanover and became a member of the rival Austro–Spanish league.

In spite of his defection, Frederick William still hankered after the double marriage even when his Hanoverian relations had made it abundantly clear that they would only consider it seriously as part of a political bargain which would restore

Prussia to the league of Hanover and align her definitely against the Hapsburgs. Seckendorff was soon able to persuade him that George II, who had succeeded his father on the British throne in 1727, was not in earnest but was merely using the double marriage project to separate him from the Emperor and thus eventually to ruin him. Sophia Dorothea, on the other hand, was so determined to bring about the double marriage that she negotiated privately with the French and British diplomatic agents at Berlin and even discussed with them the measures to be taken if her husband should die mad. Had Frederick William known, she would have been lucky to escape a charge of treason.

By this time, Frederick himself, at the age of fourteen, was closely in touch with the French diplomatic agent at Berlin and taking advice on the means of forming a crown prince's party. The king's suspicions that Frederick was plotting against him with the help of his mother and sister had thus some foundation in fact. Frederick William now gave up the double marriage and tried to coerce George II to arrange the marriage of the Prince of Wales to Wilhelmina without making any political stipulations. War with Hanover was very near in 1729 and Frederick not only undertook never to marry anyone but Princess Amelia but sent assurances of his continued friendship to George II.

When in 1730 the double marriage scheme was finally abandoned by both the British and the Prussian courts, Frederick began to consider seriously another method of ending the intolerable treatment he was suffering from his father. He confided in a young Prussian officer called Katte but before they had reached any decision Frederick William planned a visit to western Germany. While Katte was left at Berlin, the king took his eldest son on the journey with him, if only to keep him under closer observation. Frederick believed that once out of Prussia he would have a better chance to escape across the frontiers of the Empire into France, and then by easy stages to his relations in Britain. But when the time came Frederick found he was too closely guarded and his fellow conspirator, a page called Keith, proved too timid and half-hearted to make escape a practical proposition.

Finally Keith confessed to the king that he had been engaged with the crown prince in an attempt to escape to France or Holland. Frederick was arrested, beaten up and interrogated by his father who believed or pretended to believe that his son was plotting with foreign powers to murder him and seize the Prussian throne. The crown prince freely admitted his plan to escape but insisted that to remove oneself from ill-treatment, which in filial piety one could not resist, did not amount to desertion. He denied consistently that he had ever plotted against his father or engaged in intrigues with foreign powers against him. His father gave orders that his heir should be removed to Küstrin where he was kept in close confinement in the fortress, deprived of his flute, and subjected to repeated examinations.

For a time there was a possibility that the king would order the execution of his eldest son. Grumbkow and Seckendorff, who had egged him on to dismiss their opponents from all official positions, began to fear that he would over-reach himself. With their help Frederick William then decided to have his son and his fellow conspirators tried by a military tribunal, which merely reported its own incompetence to try the heir to the throne and commended him to 'his Royal Majesty's supreme and paternal mercy', but sentenced Katte to lifelong imprisonment in a fortress. Frederick William decided that justice required the death sentence on a Prussian officer who had aided and abetted the crown prince in his desertion and ordered that Katte's execution should take place at Küstrin in the presence of his fellow conspirator.

What precisely the half-mad king meant to gain is not entirely clear: he himself said that he hoped to soften Fritz's hardened heart. With this end in view Chaplain Müller who had officiated at Katte's execution was ordered by the king to 'talk, argue and pray with the Prince'. Frederick, who had fainted at the moment of his friend's execution, and at first thought the chaplain had come to prepare him to meet the same fate, soon revived sufficiently to pray for God's mercy and the king's pardon in terms which convinced Müller of his sincerity. By this time the leading sovereigns and statesmen of Europe, including the Emperor, who had a special title to interfere if the life of the heir of one of the German electors was in danger, had invoked the king's mercy for his son. Even the heads of the anti-English faction at Berlin, Grumbkow and Seckendorff, as well as the Prince of Anhalt (the old Dessauer) and other distinguished generals had all pleaded for Frederick.

Frederick William, while remaining unconvinced by Frederick's play-acting, and muttering to Grumbkow 'God grant that I may be mistaken in thinking my son is less likely to die a natural death than at the hands of the executioner', thought it better not to alienate entirely the sympathies of Europe and of his own subjects. He therefore pretended to accept at face value Müller's reports of his son's repentance. Frederick then signed a document giving up his hereditary right to the throne in the event of his again offending, and took an oath to obey without fail the king's orders as a faithful servant, subject and son. Frederick William knew that his son would never take such an oath without mental reservations, but had to content himself with the appearance of success. His real feelings about his son were privately expressed to Grumbkow: 'I hope that he won't end on the gallows yet.' Therefore, although released from confinement in the fortress of Küstrin, he was to remain in the town as a mere civilian. A deserter had lost the right to wear uniform, but could still serve the state by learning at first hand the business of provincial administration. In this way Frederick William believed he was achieving two ends—the punishment of his son, which certainly took precedence, and giving him a practical introduction to administrative problems.

Chapter Three

The Crown Prince 1730–40

FREDERICK WILLIAM, in pronouncing sentence on his son, had written that the whole town of Küstrin should be his prison. On 20 November 1730 Frederick took up his duties in the local department of war and agriculture. By the king's orders he was seated at a little table below that occupied by the civil servants with whom he was to work and when his signature was required to a document he must sign well below the signatures of colleagues. On Sundays he must attend three church services. The only books he was to be allowed to read were the Bible, the Psalter and Arndt's *True Christianity*. His own books, with a manuscript catalogue in his handwriting, had fallen into his father's hands and were sold by order at Hamburg. At first happy as a lark, Frederick soon wearied not so much of drudgery, for his office hours were only from 7 to 11.30 a.m. and 3 to 5 p.m., but of the tedium of leisure with all his favourite avocations strictly forbidden.

However, in August 1731 Frederick William paid his son a visit and though he spent most of the time railing at the crown prince, who thrice kissed his father's feet, the outcome of the visit was some relaxation of the restrictions hitherto imposed on the crown prince. He was promoted to sit at the top of the table beside the President of the department, his office hours were reduced and he was to be allowed to leave the town of Küstrin on official visits to the neighbouring royal estates and factories, provided he obtained a pass from the governor and was accompanied by an experienced civil servant. Occasionally as a treat he might even be allowed a day's hunting or a trip on the river under supervision, but he must never speak to a female. In spite of this prohibition, Frederick, now aged eighteen, seems to have conducted a literary flirtation with Louisa Eleanor von Wreech, the twenty-three-year-old wife of a Prussian colonel who lived not far from Küstrin.

Since the discovery of Frederick's plan to escape, his sister Wilhelmina had been locked up in her rooms and fed, more or less, on bread and water. Sophia Dorothea, still intent on marrying her eldest daughter to the Prince of Wales, urged Wilhelmina to take a solemn oath never to marry anyone else. Frederick William meantime rounded up three suitors, all three equally undistinguished. These were the Duke of Saxe-Weissenfels, who was middle-aged and fat, the Margrave of Schwedt, nephew of the old Dessauer, and Frederick of Brandenburg-Kulmbach, heir apparent to the Margrave of Bayreuth. If she would not marry one of the three, she would be imprisoned for life in a distant castle or convent, while her brother the crown prince would not be allowed to leave Küstrin.

Wilhelmina saw she had no option but to dissimulate and to obey her father while listening to her mother's furious curses. On 20 November 1731 she was married to the hereditary prince of Bayreuth. Her father honoured the promise he had made that Frederick should be pardoned and recalled from exile at Küstrin. When the crown prince tardily arrived at Berlin, Wilhelmina explained his obligations to her; but Frederick made it abundantly clear in private that he regarded her marriage as a *mésalliance*. The old intimacy and confidence were never really restored. Wilhelmina recorded regretfully that his caresses, such as they were, did not come from the heart. In marrying a German princeling instead of the future king of Great Britain, Wilhelmina believed that she had made a great sacrifice for the peace of her family, but she had throughout been guided primarily by selfish motives of self-preservation. Frederick was already too experienced a prince and too good a psychologist not to understand this.

Before he returned to Küstrin the crown prince had appeared at a royal review and, at the humble request of the Prussian corps of generals, he was reinstated in the army and given the rank of colonel-designate. Once returned to Küstrin he

condemned in a letter to a friend the defensive
policy of his father. The detached portions of the
Prussian dominions should be stitched together.
Neighbouring territories, especially Swedish
Pomerania, Mecklenburg and Jülich and Berg
should be added to them. In spite of all his reading, he paid little attention to historical and legal
considerations: what really moved him was
political necessity. Prince Eugene of Savoy, the
leading counsellor of the Emperor Charles VI,
when the letter was shown to him, remarked that
the young gentleman's ideas were very large and
prophesied that Frederick would one day prove
very redoubtable to his neighbours.

By this time it was clear that Frederick William,
for reasons unconnected with politics, was determined to marry off his eldest son as he had done
his eldest daughter. At the same time, through
Seckendorff and Grumbkow, Austria was pressing
him in the same direction. Charles VI had realized
the futility of his alliance with Spain. He had now
abandoned the Ostend East India Company
which had aroused the Maritime Powers to fury
and accepted gratefully Walpole's proferred
guarantee of the Pragmatic Sanction, intended to
secure the undisputed succession of his eldest
daughter to the whole of the Austrian dominions.
As early as December 1730 the Austrians were
sounding out Frederick's attitude to Elizabeth of
Brunswick-Bevern, a niece of Charles VI's wife.

Frederick at first retaliated with a circumstantial offer to marry Maria Theresa, the emperor's eldest daughter and heiress-designate, who was already virtually betrothed to the Duke of Lorraine. In the end he was, like his sister, given a choice of three spouses, but it was made clear to him that he would be well advised to choose Elizabeth.

Once again he submitted perforce to his father's wishes but stipulated that, once married, he should be given enough money to keep up an establishment of his own. He had already taken a great dislike to Elizabeth, partly because of her relatively humble birth, and did not hesitate to assert in private that she was ugly, clumsy and almost dumb. On 10 March 1732 he was formally betrothed to this monster, receiving in exchange rich presents, the resumption of his career in the army, and the promise of an establishment for himself and his bride at a reasonable distance from Berlin, where he would be out of his father's way but not out of the world.

Somewhat inexplicably in view of his anxiety to secure the succession by the birth of a grandson, Frederick William allowed more than a year to pass before his son's wedding was celebrated. Meantime Seckendorff kept Frederick supplied with ready money and had to listen to the threats the crown prince dared not make to his father: 'I will marry; but once it is over I will wish my wife

"good-day, Madam, and may luck go with you." '
The prince's attitude may help to explain the
uncertainty of the Austrian court, which led them
twice to put to Frederick William schemes for
Frederick's marriage to an English princess, but
this *volte-face* was more likely to be due to the
much improved relations between the Emperor
and Great Britain which followed upon their
reconciliation in 1731.

Frederick William naturally enough would not
hear of the revived English marriage in any shape
or form and the wedding of the crown prince and
Elizabeth of Bevern was celebrated on 12 June
1733. After a brief sojourn in the bridal bed, the
bridegroom showed himself in public and then
sat down to write to Wilhelmina: 'Thank God it's
over.'

Thankfully leaving his bride to stay with his
family, Frederick took up his new appointment as
colonel of a regiment stationed at Neu-Ruppin
about forty miles north of Berlin. He was much
occupied with his military duties and in inspecting
royal estates in the neighbourhood and suggesting
to his father ways in which more revenue could be
wrung from them. His spare time was devoted to
reading, writing and playing the flute, but as at
Küstrin he was soon bored by the lack of intellectual society. A rather reluctant father allowed him
in 1734 to see active service for the first time. It
was in the Rhineland, where the French were once

again engaged in an attack upon the Empire, that the crown prince made his first campaign, serving under Prince Eugene, the legendary hero of battles against the French and the Turks almost a generation earlier.

Recalled in October to what he expected to be his father's deathbed, it was a bitter blow to him when Frederick William recovered and refused him permission to return to the Rhineland for the campaign of 1735. Instead the crown prince was dispatched willy-nilly to pay a prolonged visit of inspection to East Prussia to make a special study of the province where his father's administrative and economic reforms had produced their greatest effect. He thus learned that this outlying, almost foreign, province of the Hohenzollern state was no Siberia, but a prosperous principality which could make a substantial contribution to the greatness of Brandenburg-Prussia.

Not far from Neu-Ruppin and a little further away than Neu-Ruppin from Berlin stood the semi-derelict castle of Rheinsberg, which Frederick, urged on and helped by his father, had bought in 1734 as a home for himself and his bride. So many alterations and improvements had to be made under the personal supervision of the crown prince that it was not until the summer of 1736 that the new owners could move in. Set on the very edge of a lake surrounded by gardens, the castle was at once elegant and cosy. Although the architect had retained one of the towers of the old building and built another to match it, the general effect was contemporary, if not commonplace. Frederick was delighted with it and amused himself by adopting the theory of the local antiquarians that Rheinsberg was a corruption of Remus-berg. He claimed that his castle stood on a site hallowed by association with the brother of Romulus, founder of Rome. It seems likely that he spent at Rheinsberg the happiest years of his life.

At last he could gather his own friends around him. Dietrich von Keyserlingk, a Courland noble, affectionately nicknamed Caesarion by the crown prince, was his closest friend. Charles Etienne Jordan, Huguenot by origin, clergyman by profession and cosmopolitan scholar by inclination, served as his secretary. Another Huguenot, Heinrich August de la Motte-Fouqué, who usually signed his name simply Fouquet as his patron the old Dessauer recommended, had some talent for amateur theatricals. Pesne, born in Paris but long resident out of his native land, and the Silesian Protestant Knobelsdorff had carried out the rebuilding and decoration of Rheinsberg and remained to enjoy and further adorn their handiwork. Soon they were joined by Algarotti, a young Venetian. Rheinsberg society was delightfully cosmopolitan, but to a Frenchified German like the crown prince there was one thing lacking—a really French Frenchman.

Rising at 4 a.m., Frederick would read for six hours on end, spend two hours in making notes on what he had read or copying out passages which had particularly impressed him. The afternoons would be spent in the same way: he seldom saw his friends except at meals or at the concerts, balls, masquerades and amateur theatricals which occupied most of his evenings. Hunting he eschewed. He even grudged himself sleep, and often stayed up reading and writing till 2 a.m. His capacity for self-education was limited only by the limits of physical endurance. All was grist that came to his mill—philosophical treatises, histories, classical and modern literature, mathematical and scientific works were devoured in turn and discussed with his friends.

And the more he read the more he wrote—letters to friends and scholars far and near, verses on endless subjects which kept occurring to him, philosophical disquisitions on the nature of God and the existence of the soul, and finally works on politics, such as his celebrated *Anti-Machiavel*. Amongst his correspondents a special place was reserved for Voltaire, to whom he addressed a letter as soon as he was established at Rheinsberg. A gracious reply from the high priest of the enlightenment rejoiced Frederick's heart. He awaited subsequent letters as a lover those of his mistress. It was not merely that he hoped to learn from his master and to bask in Voltaire's compliments: he had hopes of one day equalling if not excelling the achievements which had made Voltaire the acknowledged head of the European literary world.

At Rheinsberg Frederick discovered, somewhat to his own surprise, that women were necessary to good company, if only for their conversation. Yet he continued to neglect his wife when he was at Rheinsberg and hardly troubled to write to her when he was away from home. This was of course in accordance with the threats he had made in the interval between betrothal and marriage; but there is also some reason to believe that he was annoyed by his wife's childlessness. Even so this was the nearest approach to a normal married life that his unfortunate wife was to know. While there are certainly two sides to the quarrel between Frederick and his father, his biographers agree that his treatment of his wife is a permanent blot on his character.

A shy, timid girl, not bad looking though no beauty, not unintelligent though unable to keep pace with Frederick's impetuous rush into the enlightenment, she was as devoted to her husband as he would let her be. In spite of her husband's obvious distaste, and long after a cleverer woman would have given up the attempt, she devoted herself wholeheartedly to making a success of her marriage. A truly enlightened prince living in the age of Reason might surely have recognized that if he had been forced to marry her she had been forced to marry him.

Apart from his undoubted personal resentment, it has often been suggested that Frederick's treatment of his wife was symptomatic of deeper maladjustment. In view of the recorded facts about the family of Hohenzollern, it is tempting to regard him as basically homosexual, though there seems to be no adequate evidence of this in Frederick's case. Soon after his death a Swiss physician asserted that Frederick, as a result of sexual intercourse at Dresden with one of Augustus the Strong's mistresses, had contracted a disease which had been so unskilfully treated by his doctors that he was thenceforth impotent. This was at once denied by several of the royal physicians resident in Prussia, though how much weight should be attached to their evidence is a nice matter.

Whatever the truth may be, from this time onwards women played no part in Frederick's life. Almost his first act after his succession to the throne was to forbid his wife to follow him from Berlin to Charlottenburg and thereafter they were rarely under the same roof. He found it very useful to have a wife whom he need not see. As long as she lived, and in the end she survived him, there could be no talk of his remarriage.

Even when he was intent at Rheinsberg on making his name as a man of letters, Frederick was fully aware that it was much more important that he should prepare himself in every possible way for the trade of king which must soon be his. Himself destitute of any deep religious convictions, he recognized the political value of Protestantism to the German princes, and partly because of the long drawn out argument with his father on the doctrine of the elect, he preferred Calvinist to Lutheran theology. While denouncing the intolerance of religious sects and preaching the universal toleration which comes easily to the indifferent, his own approach to the Church was markedly Erastian. Once he had succeeded to the throne religion was never more to him than a useful tool to the politician.

As a young man Frederick had been much impressed by the metaphysics of Leibniz as expounded by his pupil Wolff, but at Rheinsberg this gave way to the scepticism of Bayle and Voltaire. Chance took the place assigned earlier to Providence in his metaphysical system; but even in a world governed by chance he believed that human activity, directed by prudence and foresight, availed much. At this point Frederick's historical studies came to his aid. Disbelieving in primitive liberty and equality of men, Frederick recognized all forms of government as legitimate. The past history of Brandenburg-Prussia, and the absence of political forces capable of standing up to the monarchy, pointed to absolute monarchy as the natural form of government for Prussia. This did not mean that the ruler should be absolute master of his subjects—did the ominous shadow of his father fall on the philosopher of Rheinsberg's mind as he wrote this passage? On the contrary the prince must be the first servant of the state. But if he was to be able to serve the state effectually he must have absolute freedom to do his subjects good. Unfortunately absolute freedom to do good carried with it unfettered ability to do ill; and Frederick had read enough history to realize how rare were kings who did not abuse their powers.

For himself he had already decided upon his course. Incessant activity, mental and physical, was required of the first servant of the state, but he must first know in his own mind where he was going if he was to make good use of the ever-changing circumstances around him. Frederick at this stage in his career, disclaimed 'the primacy of foreign policy': justice, under which term he included administration and internal policy, came first. Though he put second the military duties of the prince, a prince who is not a soldier in his opinion is only half a prince. Not only were defensive wars legitimate, as were wars waged to maintain rights and claims essential to the state, but even preventative wars undertaken by a far-sighted prince to avoid future dangers. Indeed when a war broke out in his neighbourhood, a wise prince would never remain neutral but would join in the struggle: by remaining neutral he risked everything and could expect to gain nothing. On the other hand nothing was more fatal to a prince than an excessive desire for military glory, witness Charles XII of Sweden. War, however, was not the only way to make conquests: a laborious prince who made the arts and sciences flourish in his dominions and thereby improved their organization and their economy, brought out their potential strength.

It will be apparent to the reader that Frederick's ideas were essentially derivative, though he was good at phrase-making. His greatness lay in action, not in metaphysical speculation nor even in political thought. Still the years of self-education for the work of government were not lost, indeed they provided the indispensable basis for his reign. Few princes on their accession to a throne have been so thoroughly imbued with the spirit of their own age. Fewer still have known so precisely where they were going or what they must do to get there. Having thrown divine right monarchy overboard, Frederick knew he must depend on his own exertions. God—or Chance—would no doubt give him opportunities and he felt competent to seize and exploit them.

Chapter Four

The First Two Silesian Wars
1740-45

THE charm of Rheinsberg for Frederick was the separation from his father and the ability to live his own life. Once or twice the king paid the young couple a mercifully short visit; much oftener the crown prince was summoned to his father's court or to play his part in a review. He would be received with affection but soon the king's humour would change. He would criticize his son gently, proceed to denounce Rheinsberg and all its ways and end up by railing at him for not providing a direct heir to the throne. Frederick dared not answer back but continued to profess submission and penitence. After one of these scenes Frederick said he wished he could beg his bread abroad. Even when he was at home, the king kept him chronically short of cash and forced him to borrow money right and left.

Apart from the meaningless professions, which had become habitual, Frederick found the best way to propitiate his father was to secure tall recruits for his regiment, fit them out with particularly smart uniforms and see that their parade ground drill was impeccable. It was after one of these exhibitions that Frederick William, in a rare access of good humour, publicly told his son 'There is a Frederick William in you after all'. On another such occasion, despondent over the failure of his foreign policy and furious at the contemptuous way in which both Austria and France were treating him, he pointed to his heir and burst out: 'There goes one who will avenge me'.

When the old king died on 31 May 1740 everyone expected a complete change of men and measures at the Prussian court. Frederick did indeed invite his friends, those of Rheinsberg and those of even older and unhappier days, to his court and gave to each what the new king of Prussia regarded as a suitable reward. In all cases this was much less than his old friends had expected and he made it abundantly clear that they need not expect to have any share in shaping the policies of the new reign. Even Caesarion was told bluntly that Frederick valued him as a courtier and soldier but considered him a fool as a politician.

On the other hand Leopold of Anhalt-Dessau, nicknamed the Old Dessauer, was allowed to keep the offices which he and his sons had held under Frederick William I, but was told with equal bluntness he would no longer be allowed to meddle with policy. His father's ministers remained in office: they had made their peace with Frederick before his accession. Even Grumbkow had for years received Frederick's political confidences and so far as he dared had acted as middleman between him and his father. On Grumbkow's death his place had been taken by his son-in-law Podewils. Frederick kept the old ministers in office but reserved all decisions to himself, as his father had done or at least intended to do. Each minister severally reported and made proposals to the king, who then sent him the royal orders. This was the cabinet system of government as it came to be understood in Prussia. Within a few weeks of his accession, he told his ministers that though they might understand negotiations they knew no more about war than an Iroquois Indian about astronomy.

There was of course some window dressing at the beginning of the new reign: Frederick knew that it was important to create an attractive public image of his government. Instead of chasing his subjects about the streets of Berlin, belabouring them with his cane and screaming at them 'Love me, scum', he issued a few enlightened edicts. Torture as a part of the judicial process as well as the censorship of the press were officially abolished and religious toleration proclaimed. The king took the chair at a meeting of freemasons. The Berlin Academy of Sciences was reconstituted and distinguished scholars invited to join it, notably

Euler and Maupertuis. Even in the army some minor reforms were announced and the regiment of giants was disbanded. Many of the royal hunting grounds were deforested and devoted to more profitable economic use. But the keynote of the new reign was struck not in a public declaration but in the king's orders to his ministers, that instead of basing their policies and actions on an assumed separation between the interests of the king and those of the country, they must henceforth act on Frederick's own maxim that the king's interest consisted solely in securing the advantage and happiness of his people. Discarding the outworn trappings of the Holy Roman Empire and the *mystique* of anointment with holy oil, and remarking that a crown was just a hat that lets the rain in, he took the title of *rex Borussorum*, king of the Prussians, not as his two predecessors had been, *rex Borussiae*, king merely of that detached fragment of the Hohenzollern territories far to the east of Brandenburg.

In the opening months of his reign it seemed that in foreign policy also Frederick would continue in the path followed by his father. His envoys at foreign courts were instructed to try to secure recognition of the Prussian claims to the Rhenish fiefs of Jülich and Berg, which had been the main preoccupation of Frederick William for the greater part of his reign. He himself went for a tour in western Germany to meet Voltaire near

Cleve, visit Wilhelmina at Bayreuth and for the only time in his life set foot on French soil. This brief visit to Strassburg and personal contact with the French in their own country left him with an unfavourable impression—

> *Superbe en sa fortune, en sa maleur rampant,*
> *D'un bavardage impitoyable*
> *Pour cacher le creux d'un esprit ignorant.*

But already Frederick had settled in his own favour a long-standing quarrel over the county of Herstal which was eager to escape from the conscription and financial exactions of the Hohenzollerns to the milder rule of the neighbouring prince bishop of Liège. Unimpressed by the threats of France and Austria, Frederick marched a few thousand Prussians into the diocese and forced the bishop to buy Herstal from him at his own price.

Then came news of the deaths in rapid succession of the Emperor Charles VI and of the Tsaritsa Anne. Frederick's hour of destiny had come sooner than he could have expected and he was ready to seize it with both hands. Under Charles VI the prestige and power of the Hapsburgs had markedly declined and in the closing years of his reign his armies had been defeated and dispirited. His ministers were old and incapable. There was formidable discontent even in the hereditary Hapsburg lands, while garrisons had to be scattered for the protection and policing of distant parts of the dominions. The Magyars in particular were waiting for a chance to overthrow their German masters. In spite of the almost complete acceptance within and without the Empire of the celebrated Pragmatic Sanction, intended to secure the undisputed acceptance of Charles's eldest daughter, Maria Theresa, as ruler of the Hapsburg lands, there was certain to be opposition to her accession from various competitors. Two daughters of Charles VI's elder brother, Joseph I, one married to the Bavarian and the other to the Saxon Elector, would certainly put forward claims, while Savoy and Spain would try to gain Austrian territory in Italy. Moreover the death of Charles VI meant the election of a new Holy Roman Emperor and even if France stuck to the bargain she had made with Charles VI and allowed Maria Theresa to succeed to all the Hapsburg lands, she was certain to oppose the election of Maria Theresa's husband, Francis Stephen of Lorraine and now Grand-duke of Tuscany, as Emperor.

Frederick had already analysed the situation in a masterly way. As he saw it, the death of Anne of Russia, followed by acute internal dissension at the court of her infant successor, removed the last impediment to complete freedom of action for Prussia. Deprived of effective Russian support, Maria Theresa could hardly refuse the terms he had already decided to offer her in exchange for his help against her rivals, who would be certain to have the sympathy if not the support of France. His price was the cession of certain territories in the Austrian province of Silesia to which the Hohenzollerns had periodically asserted claims for nearly a century.

Leaving his ministers and especially Podewils to draw up and send to Maria Theresa a statement of these claims from the voluminous files in the foreign office, he led his troops into Silesia. A more prudent prince would have waited for the coalition to form and, after joining it, would have worked to secure his own ends. Frederick preferred, now as throughout his career, to act first and negotiate afterwards. Wherever the Prussian troops went, they dispersed broadsheets which proclaimed that Frederick was marching to help Maria Theresa to defend her dominions against her many enemies. Perhaps more important was the promise to free the Lutheran protestants, long oppressed by Hapsburg fanaticism, from an intolerable yoke, but without shifting their disabilities on to the shoulders of the Catholic majority. Neither Protestant nor Catholic had any particular affection for their Austrian overlord. Merchant and peasant were glad to sell supplies for ready money to the invaders and Frederick kept his troops under strict discipline.

By this time Maria Theresa had indignantly

rejected Frederick's demands and was laboriously
collecting troops from other parts of her dominions
to reinforce the Silesian garrisons, which could
only muster 3,000 men against the 40,000 Prussians which Frederick brought with him. The
Imperial city of Breslau, which was also the
Austrian administrative headquarters for Silesia,
opened its gates to the invaders, thankfully
accepting Frederick's offer of neutrality in what
was unmistakably becoming an Austro–Prussian
war. By the middle of January 1741 practically
the whole of Silesia, apart from a few fortress-
towns garrisoned by pitifully small Austrian
garrisons, was in Prussian hands.

Not until the beginning of April had the
Austrians gathered sufficient troops for a counter-
invasion of Silesia. Crossing the mountains from
Bohemia in a blizzard, the Austrian general
Neipperg threatened the Prussian bases in Lower
Silesia. Frederick gave battle at Mollwitz (10
April). The Austrian cavalry utterly routed the
Prussian horse in spite of Frederick's reckless
exposure of himself in the mêlée. His generals,
more afraid of their responsibility for his safety
than of the Austrians, advised him to leave the
stricken field and then used the terrible Prussian
infantry, drilled by Frederick William and the
Old Dessauer, to sweep away the motley Austrian
brigades of infantry, while the Austrian cavalry
had disappeared from the battlefield and could

not be concentrated in time to give support to their infantry against the Prussian onslaught.

Meantime Frederick had outdistanced his escort, narrowly escaped capture by the Austrians and finally turned up forty-eight hours later not far from the battlefield to find that his generals had won the first Prussian victory in the field since the days of the Great Elector. In later life he tried to conceal his mortification by claiming that Mollwitz served as a school for himself and his army.

At the time, since Austria was universally regarded as a Great Power and Prussia as a minor one, Mollwitz caused a sensation in Europe. The powers which had been inclined to support Austria reconsidered the situation. The claimants to the Austrian succession all counted their chickens before they were hatched. France decided to take the opportunity of Frederick's victory to destroy once and for all Austrian domination of the Empire and, along with Spain, signed the treaty of Nymphenburg (May 1741) with the leading claimant to Maria Theresa's inheritance, Charles Albert of Bavaria.

Frederick joined the league of Nymphenburg in June, promising to vote for Charles Albert as Emperor and receiving in exchange a French guarantee of Lower Silesia and French promises to send an army into Germany to divert Austria's attention, and to stir up Sweden to attack Russia and thus avert any danger of Russia threatening East Prussia. The Franco–Bavarian army advanced down the Danube, but turned aside from Vienna when it was at their mercy and began to occupy Bohemia.

Even now Maria Theresa, realizing she could not successfully oppose France and Prussia at the same time, would have preferred to buy off France and concentrate her available forces against Prussia. France would have none of it, so Maria Theresa under British mediation concluded the convention of Klein Schellendorf (October 1741) with Frederick. This was in effect a secret armistice, to be concealed from the other belligerents by a sham siege of Neisse, the most important Austrian base in Silesia, at the end of which Neisse would be surrendered to Frederick. This enabled Maria Theresa with the aid of Neipperg's troops and a new Hungarian army to overrun Bavaria and isolate the French in Bohemia.

Austrian successes so alarmed Frederick that he denounced the convention of Klein Schellendorf and attacked the Austrian province of Moravia. Here he made little progress and after winning the battle of Chotusitz in the valley of the Elbe (May 1742) withdrew for the second time from the struggle. Chotusitz was the first of Frederick's personal victories and by the preliminary treaty of Breslau, confirmed a month later by the definitive treaty of Berlin (July 1742), Frederick gained nearly the whole of Silesia, except Teschen, as well as the neighbouring county of Glatz. In exchange he accepted responsibility for servicing and repaying a loan raised by Charles VI from an international *consortorium* on the security of the Silesian revenues.

Once again he had promised to remain neutral in the Franco–Austrian war and the British government, which had pressed Maria Theresa to accept Frederick's terms, had hopes of winning him over permanently from the French to the British camp. Indeed Carteret had only secured Maria Theresa's signature by promising her compensation elsewhere for the loss of Silesia and 1743–4 saw an Anglo-Austrian attempt to retain Bavaria and reconquer Alsace from the Bourbons. Frederick dared not allow Maria Theresa to oppress his former Bavarian ally, now Holy Roman Emperor and a landless wanderer—*et Caesar et nihil*. Still less could he afford to see the complete defeat of France and Austrian domination of Germany.

In June 1744 he renewed his alliance with France and marched into Bohemia. While his basic motive was no doubt the protection of Silesia, he had secured from the Bavarian emperor a written promise that he could retain certain territories in Bohemia, always provided he could conquer them. Austria, with her resources overstretched in distant campaigns, had to watch the

Prussians occupying the whole of Bohemia in a few weeks. But Frederick knew well he could only maintain himself in Bohemia if the French took a vigorous part in the renewed German war.

Not unreasonably in view of his desertions of France, the French deliberately let him down. The Austrian armies were allowed to withdraw from Alsace, cross the Rhine unopposed and make for Bohemia unpursued. There they came under the command of Traun, the only first-class general opposed to Frederick in the whole of the two Silesian wars. Traun refused to fight a pitched battle with the Prussians, outmanoeuvred Frederick and forced him stage by stage to evacuate Bohemia.

Then came the death of the Emperor Charles VII (January 1745). His son Maximilian Joseph was thankful to abandon his father's claims and to receive back from Austria the Bavarian electorate. This at one and the same time deprived Frederick of his claim to be acting as a champion of the imperial constitution and the rights of the princes and made Maria Theresa more determined than ever to recover Silesia, since she could no longer hope to keep Bavaria as compensation for the loss of Silesia. Also the Saxon elector, who had begun as a claimant to the Austrian succession and had hovered uncertainly from side to side, was now bribed by the Maritime Powers in his jealousy of

Prussian success to assist Maria Theresa to recover Silesia.

Unfortunately for herself, Maria Theresa entrusted this invasion not to Traun, who was sent to make certain of her husband's election as emperor at Frankfurt, but to her brother-in-law, Charles of Lorraine, whose record of failure was already outstanding even for an Austrian general. Charles was defeated at Hohenfriedberg and Soor but Maria Theresa was a glutton for punishment. Finally Frederick sent the Old Dessauer into Saxony, where he won the battle of Kesselsdorf, occupied Dresden and knocked Saxony out of the war. Maria Theresa, deprived of the Saxon auxiliaries, bullied by Britain and fearing to lose her territories in Italy and the Netherlands to France and Spain, made peace at Dresden (December 1745). So far as Austria and Prussia were concerned the treaty of Dresden simply confirmed the treaty of Berlin which had ended the first Silesian war.

Though the war of the Austrian Succession was to continue for another three years Frederick took no further part in it. He had won fame and had proved himself both as soldier and statesman—already men at Berlin and elsewhere were giving him the title of Frederick the Great. Although the Prussian troops had proved as excellent on the battlefield as on the parade ground, the acquisition of Silesia, solemnly guaranteed to Prussia by all the belligerents by the treaty of Aix-la-Chapelle (1748), was due more to Frederick's skilful exploitation of the international situation than to his victories in battle. When he wrote in his *Memoirs* that two years of war sufficed to win this important province for Prussia, he was well aware than even after 1748 his tenure of Silesia was contingent and precarious.

On the other hand the treaty of Dresden, so long as Frederick could keep possession of Silesia, marked the beginning of a new era in German politics. The Hohenzollerns had raised themselves from the vassalage to the Emperor which had so infuriated Frederick William and had finally outdistanced their competitors, the Welfs of Hanover, the Wettins of Saxony and the Wittelsbachs of Bavaria. Henceforth for a century and a quarter, until the proclamation at Versailles of the Hohenzollern *Reich* in 1871, there were to be two military monarchies within the Empire and Confederation, contending with each other on more or less equal terms. The period of dualism in German politics had begun.

These changes inevitably had repercussions in Europe. France had never wanted to destroy Austria. The emergence of a rival German power to Austria suited her admirably, since by playing off Austria and Prussia against each other she might be able to dominate Germany. Britain on the other hand had vainly sought to bring Austria and Prussia together throughout the war in the hope of persuading them to cooperate against France. British ministers believed that the war proved that Britain, with the lethargic Dutch in tow, and allied to Austria, was not strong enough to resist successfully the house of Bourbon and its allies. When Dutch resistance collapsed in 1747–8 and Austria was too busy in Italy to reinforce her troops in the Netherlands, Britain appealed to Frederick for help. The King of Prussia professed willingness to take the place of Austria as Britain's continental partner, but absolutely declined to join the Austro–British old system. Nothing therefore came of this approach at the time; but Frederick may rightly be regarded as the first European statesman to see the need for the Diplomatic Revolution.

If the acquisition of Silesia went far to determine the political significance of Frederick's reign, it was almost as important economically to Prussia. Frederick hesitated at first between treating Silesia as an underdeveloped colonial province which should be encouraged to produce raw materials for processing in the more advanced provinces of Prussia or as a region with valuable craft-industries which should be further developed by the state. During the Seven Years War, in spite of the contending armies, Silesia continued to produce large quantities of woollen cloth and was the only Prussian province which could pay its taxes regularly during the war. The loss of markets in Austria was compensated by expansion in exports of cloth to Poland.

Frederick was also anxious to develop the mining of iron and other ores which had long been exploited on a small scale in parts of Silesia. New blast furnaces were started at Malapane and Kreuzburg just in time to help production of armaments in the Seven Years War. The setting up of a mining department for Silesia in 1769 and the energetic pioneering work of Friedrich Anton von Heinitz and Friedrich Wilhelm von Reden soon established coalmining, ironworking and leadmining and smelting on an extensive scale. Success came after Frederick's death, but the original impetus was due to him and he deliberately used Silesia as a testing ground for experiments which could be adapted to meet the needs of other Prussian provinces, particularly the Ruhr, which were endowed with large-scale mineral deposits.[1]

[1] This and the preceding paragraph are based on W. O. Henderson, *The State and the Industrial Revolution in Prussia* 1740–1870 (Liverpool U.P., 1958).

Chapter Five

The Ten Years Peace 1746–56

DURING the wars Frederick and his favourite sister Wilhelmina had been quarrelling bitterly with each other. The Margravine of Bayreuth lived in the Austrian sphere of influence and dared not openly support her brother, who was furious when he heard that she had visited Frankfurt and personally congratulated Maria Theresa on Francis I's election as Holy Roman Emperor in succession to Frederick's friend and protégé, Charles VII. Worse still, the authorities at Bayreuth had allowed a journalist at Erlangen, the second town in the Margraviate of Bayreuth, to publish a long series of violent attacks upon Frederick.

The treaty of Dresden restored political harmony between brother and sister. Wilhelmina, whose own marriage had gone on the rocks, visited her brother twice in 1750 and tried to make a third in the relationship between Frederick and Voltaire, who habitually referred to her as the Abbess of Bayreuth and wrote to invoke her mediation in his quarrel with her brother. During the earlier years of the Seven Years War the situation was reversed and Frederick appealed to his sister to assist him in his futile attempts to arrange a separate peace with France. When Wilhelmina died in October 1758, at a time when Frederick's cause seemed hopeless, he was more affected by her death than by the military disaster at Hochkirch. Perhaps it would be true to say that in mourning for her he mourned his own lost youth.

Long before the death of Wilhelmina he had deliberately excluded his wife from his life. His mother, after his accession to the throne, he had treated with a distant respect until her death in 1757. Henceforth no woman had any significant place in his thoughts. Jordan and Keyserlingk, the closest of his Rheinsberg friends, had both died in 1745. His most valued business associates were now his political secretary Eichel and his foreign minister Podewils, son-in-law of Grumbkow, but neither ever took the place of his dead friends.

The nearest approach to an intimate friend that the king now had was his chamberlain Fredersdorff. Originally a common soldier but an uncommonly good flautist, Fredersdorff had been sent by General Schwerin to relieve the tedium of Frederick's imprisonment at Küstrin. Like Frederick himself he became a freemason. Serving as the crown prince's valet in the Rheinsberg days, he won the complete confidence of his master. With Fredersdorff Frederick felt no need to pose. The hundreds of letters written in execrable German by the king to his servant and friend which have survived prove the tender, almost maternal, solicitude of Fredersdorff's master. In October 1740, when Frederick was lying ill with fever, it was Fredersdorff and not Podewils or Eichel who ventured to break to him the news that the Emperor Charles VI was dead. His official title was chamberlain to the king but Voltaire better described his functions as those of the king's factotum. As early as 1741 Frederick listed him among his six best friends. He had no political role but his death in 1758 severed almost the last link between the carefree days at Rheinsberg, as they must have seemed in retrospect, and the almost insupportable burdens of the Seven Years War.

Instead of human beings, Frederick was already, in 1745, turning for companionship and devotion to dogs and particularly to the whippet bitches which constantly accompanied him on his travels. When one of them fell into enemy hands along with the rest of the king's baggage during the battle of Soor, Frederick wept tears of joy when she was returned to him safe and sound. He did not say so, but the more he saw of human beings, the more he preferred dogs. One of the last things he did on his deathbed was to tell his servants to put a rug over one of his dogs which he thought showed signs of being cold. Had his own wishes

been carried out, he would have been buried near
his dogs on the terrace at Sans Souci.

In some ways the most significant of Frederick's
relationships during the ten years peace was that
with Voltaire. As crown prince at Rheinsberg he
had corresponded regularly with his idol in terms
which seem excessive to the twentieth century but
were not out of keeping with the literary conventions of Frederick's day. Almost his first act when
his father's death gave him personal freedom was
to arrange a meeting with Voltaire near Cleve in
September 1740.

> The two men had much in common: energy,
> wit, malice, love of literature, interest in philo-
> sophical speculation, a gift for intrigue, im-
> patience with stupidity and contempt for
> supernatural religion. There were times when
> Voltaire distrusted Frederick and when
> Frederick despised Voltaire, and there were
> times when both had good reasons for their
> feelings. But each knew his friend and the world
> well enough to appreciate the other's virtues,
> although never as much as the other's vices.[1]

Although Frederick had long wanted to 'pos-
sess' Voltaire, it was not until the summer of 1750
that he finally persuaded his pen friend to come to
Berlin to reside as he hoped permanently at his
court. Voltaire's friends in France spoke of this as

[1] Peter Gay, *Voltaire's Politics* (Princeton U.P., 1959), p. 148.

desertion. Attempts were even made to turn him into a French spy at Berlin. On the other hand Frederick forged a letter from Voltaire full of witticisms at the expense of the French king and his courtiers and let it fall into the hands of the French government with the avowed object of making it impossible for Voltaire ever to return to France.

Voltaire, whose avarice was notorious, then tried to use his inside knowledge to speculate on the Berlin bourse and became involved in a law-suit with his banker at Berlin. Finally Voltaire openly intervened in a quarrel between two members of the Berlin Academy in favour of the member who did not have Frederick's support. When he followed this up with a lampoon against Maupertuis, the President of the Berlin Academy, Frederick had the pamphlet burned by the common hangman and the ashes sent to Maupertuis. Frederick had squeezed the orange and now threw away the peel to use his own words. Voltaire left Berlin in March 1753 and never met Frederick again, although they renewed their correspondence on the outbreak of the Seven Years War and continued to correspond intermittently until Voltaire died in 1778.

Even during the years when his intimacy with Frederick was at its height, Voltaire had no influence upon the king of Prussia's statecraft. Though Voltaire paid him a visit when he was planning the invasion of Silesia, Frederick kept his own counsel. During the Silesian wars Voltaire vainly preached peace and, if forced into war, the utilitarian advantages of not deserting one's allies, particularly France. Even in the more theoretical sphere of enlightened absolutism, it is hard to attribute any specific influence on Frederick's ideas to Voltaire. Religious toleration, abolition of torture and economic development were already part of his mental furniture. They were part of the *Zeitgeist*: Frederick did not owe them to Voltaire or the *philosophes*, but it pleased him to find that his ideas coincided so far with theirs that his actions could be justified in accordance with the most enlightened social theories of the day.

While he recognized that he needed Voltaire's help as a literary adviser, what he expected in politics was simply Voltaire's endorsement of his own principles and actions. It did not take Voltaire long to discover after his arrival in Berlin that Frederick had greatly embellished Sparta, but had transported Athens only into his own study. Frederick for his part remarked of Voltaire in 1754 that he was good to read but dangerous to meet. It may not have been without influence on their quarrel that Voltaire, instead of devoting all his time at Berlin to writing panegyrics on Frederick, spent much of his leisure finishing his *Siècle de Louis XIV*. David Hume remarked with his usual acuteness that Frederick's own literary pretensions made him 'too much a rival to be a very constant patron'.[1]

In fact Frederick's patronage extended far beyond the literary world. Before the second Silesian war was over, his architect friend, Knobelsdorff had built for him the Berlin Opera House. The old castle of the Hohenzollerns at Potsdam was reconstructed, added to and embellished with pilasters, colonnades, balustrades and statues. Internally Frederick gutted the apartments occupied by his father and replaced them with rooms which sought to reproduce in a very different, urban setting the charming chambers of Rheinsberg. About the same time Knobelsdorff added a wing to Frederick's grandmother's palace at Charlottenburg where he sometimes lived in the intervals between his campaigns. He soon found that Charlottenburg was too near Berlin, a place of unhappy memories, while his privacy was disturbed by crowds of sightseers and petitioners.

In the midst of the second Silesian war he decided to build for himself an entirely new residence which should mirror his own exquisite taste and provide exactly the right background for the life of a philosopher-king. The site was already available at Potsdam quite near the castle on a piece of ground which his father had used partly to grow vegetables for the royal kitchens, partly for recreation in the summer months. Frederick

[1] *Letters of David Hume*, ed. Greig I, 207.

began by ordering that this ground should be terraced and planted with vines. He rejected Knobelsdorff's plan to build, perched on the top of the hill, overlooking the town and the river Havel, a castle in the Rheinsberg style.

For this romantic vision, Frederick substituted a small single-storeyed building well back from the edge of the hill overlooking the terraces, and surrounded with ornamental trees and clipped hedges which gave complete seclusion to its royal architect. The rooms that the king would himself use were grouped on the left, those intended for visitors on the right. Between them was an oval dining room where in the evenings he would play the host and display his talents to a select circle of enlightened and deferential friends. His own apartments included a picture gallery, a library, a music room and a bedroom, as well as the audience chamber for receiving the few official visitors that Frederick allowed to come to Potsdam on business. The best-known architectural feature of the new summer palace was the front which faced the gardens. In varying attitudes, rather weary carya-tids supported a heavy cornice on which rested a balustrade embellished with urns.

Begun in January 1745, the structure was almost complete by the end of the year, when the treaty of Dresden allowed Frederick to concentrate upon the decoration and furnishing of the interior. Frederick preferred white and pastel colours. The rooms were adorned with elaborate mantelpieces hung with tapestries and furnished with costly velvets, brocades and silks. Everywhere there was a profusion of silver and gilt ornamentation: the pictures in the picture gallery were Lancrets and Watteaus. Busts and statues, vases and marble tables were everywhere in the palace and soon spread outwards to the terrace and the garden. Many of them had formed part of the Polignac collection of antiques which Frederick had purchased some years earlier and was now able to show off to advantage. The whole inspiration and much of the workmanship and materials were French, as was to be expected from Frederick, yet the completed work is rightly regarded as a masterpiece of German rococo. Try as he would, Frederick could no more master the delicacy and restraint of French architecture and interior decoration than the finer points of French verse.

Sans Souci, the king's own name for the new palace, was ready for occupation in the summer of 1747. Henceforth it was his favourite place of residence and he continued for long to embellish it. New pictures, statues, hangings and furniture were commissioned for it and new buildings, including a Greek temple, a Chinese pavilion and a shell grotto, were erected in the grounds. Frederick devoted much attention to his gardens and was constantly trying experiments: here alone English influence was stronger than French.

Historians and art critics have sometimes wondered why Frederick did not use Sans Souci as a medium for self-glorification. Since no one could describe him as a modest man, the answer is presumably that he recognized a distinction between himself as the victorious king and as the follower of the Muses. Sans Souci was to be a retreat from the cares of state and there was no need to try to impress official and especially foreign visitors whom he was determined to keep at a distance. The first seven years of his reign cover all Frederick's achievements as architect and builder with the single exception of the new palace which he began to build at Berlin as soon as the Seven Years War ended.

His addiction to music on the other hand lasted as long as his life. He never lost his childhood passion for the flute. Wilhelmina and he had often found consolation in music for the harshness and ill-temper of their father and the brutality of his servants. He tried his hand as a composer from time to time, and one of his symphonies was in 1963 played on the Third Programme in Britain. The jubilant victor of Hohenfriedberg composed a march to celebrate his triumph. He loved to attend the operas which were performed in the opera house which he built at Berlin. To secure the services of La Barberina as a ballet dancer, Frederick put pressure on Venice where she was performing, and had her transported virtually as a prisoner to Berlin in 1744. Once there, the new star enjoyed a professional triumph and many privileges, while the gossips asserted that Frederick himself was one of her numerous lovers. For four years she appeared in the Berlin opera, received a colossal salary and was often included in Frederick's supper parties. Then she fell into disfavour for daring to marry Chancellor Cocceji's son and Berlin saw her no more.

But it was always literature which occupied most of Frederick's spare time, even during the first two Silesian wars. When he had concluded the treaty of Dresden he declared that henceforth he would not even attack a cat except in self-defence. Yet he continued to study the art of war; and, inspired by a meeting with Maurice de Saxe, the ablest and most successful commander on the French side in the War of the Austrian Succession, he wrote a French poem, *L'Art de la guerre*. This was not meant merely as an exercise in French verse composition. Frederick believed that the best way to get up a subject was to write a book about it. He was in fact trying to reduce to a system the lessons he had learned about strategy and tactics in the war of the Austrian succession.

Frederick submitted his verses on the art of war to Voltaire for expert advice with results which have recently been examined by the leading authority on Voltaire, Theodore Besterman. Out of 1,600 lines in the whole poem over 300 were actually composed or completely recast by Voltaire and inserted by Frederick in the published poem. Voltaire was also a severe critic of many other lines, phrases and words used by the royal poetaster. Besterman conjectures that his freedom may well have contributed to the temporary breach between the king of the philosophers and his royal pupil of Prussia.

More successful both for its contents and its style was Frederick's *Histoire de mon temps* in which he gave in French prose his version of the first two Silesian wars. A convinced believer that history is the best school for princes, he spent nearly as much effort on explaining where and why he had erred as in justifying his policies and magnifying his successes. Subsequently Frederick wrote similar accounts of his later wars and diplomacy. All these historical memoirs were included in the edition of Frederick's works published shortly after his death. Ever since they have been recognized as one of the basic sources for the life of Frederick and the rise of Prussia.

Eminently quotable, they have been plundered by successive generations of historians and have become known to the many students of eighteenth-century Europe who would never think of reading an original text. While the element of propaganda is pervasive and unmistakable, Frederick's memoirs give a much more accurate and balanced narrative than the equally celebrated, but unreliable, *Reflections and Reminiscences* of Bismarck. His appearance of candour and his moderation in pleading his own cause often carry conviction. The French editor of the edition in which they are usually read did not hesitate to compare them to Caesar's *Commentaries*. This tribute would have charmed Frederick, who remarked sweepingly in 1775 that history after Caesar consisted solely of panegyric and satire.

It was also during the truce between the second and third of Frederick's Silesian wars that his own ideas on government were most clearly revealed. He may have worked even harder at the reconstruction of his kingdom after the Seven Years War, but the basic ideas had been adumbrated and nearly all of them tried out in practice in the decade from 1746 to 1756. It is true to say that except in the sphere of justice he changed little and that many of his modifications of his father's system did not endure.

Under Frederick William the keystone of the administrative arch had been the General Directory, divided into four departments, each responsible for a group of provinces. No decision could be taken by the departmental head except in conjunction with his colleagues in the other departments. In addition to administrative control of a group of provinces each head of department often directed for the whole kingdom a specialized agency of government, such as the post office. Procedure was strictly regulated from above by the king's written instructions, reinforced by the 'collegiate system'. Below were the seventeen provincial chambers, also collegiate in structure, and absolutely controlled by the General Directory. And under the provincial chambers were local commissaries in rural districts (*Steuerräte*) and municipal magistrates in the towns, all completely subordinated to the next rank in the administrative hierarchy.

All decisions came from above. What was required in the lower ranges was not initiative but implicit obedience and unremitting industry. On the other hand there was no sign of the operation of Parkinson's law in eighteenth-century Prussia. Even at the end of Frederick's reign the whole civil service did not exceed 14,000 men, considerably less than a tenth of the strength of the Prussian army.

Frederick maintained to the day of his death the peculiar Prussian system of cabinet government which his father had perfected. In contemporary Britain this would have been described as government in the royal closet. It meant government by the king, aided by one or two confidential secretaries. The most important of these was Eichel, who had served a ten years' apprenticeship under Frederick William. These secretaries transmitted the king's orders to the ministers in charge of the various departments of government. Frederick had even less respect for his ministers and their opinions than his father had had for his. If he no longer, like his father, belaboured an erring minister with his cane, he lashed him with his tongue. Even Podewils, who was for long his foreign minister and served the king faithfully and well, when he ventured to remonstrate timidly against Frederick's invasion of Saxony in 1756, was dismissed with the sneer *'Adieu, monsieur de la timide politique'*.

Year in, year out, the greater part of Frederick's working day, and it usually began at 5 a.m., was devoted to routine work, the reading and annotating of dispatches from his diplomatic agents, reports and queries from his ministers, letters from his generals and provincial administrators and petitions from the local nobility. So far as humanly possible, all had been dealt with by midday. Then the royal decisions were prepared by his secretaries, examined by the king the same afternoon and immediately communicated to those concerned. The rest of the day was devoted to the cultivation of the Muses and to conversation and recreation with his friends. As Voltaire put it

> *Il est grand roi tout le matin,*
> *Après diner grand écrivain,*
> *Tout le jour philosophe humain*
> *Et le soir convive divin.*

In summer when Frederick normally inspected his kingdom, province by province, and even in autumn when he was chiefly occupied with the military manoeuvres he judged necessary to keep his army constantly at fighting pitch, the same daily routine was observed.

Only a man of superhuman industry could have kept this system operating with reasonable efficiency as Frederick continued to do. In hurriedly reading a document dealing with technical matters. Frederick sometimes missed the point altogether or made what was clearly a bad choice between two alternatives. Yet he retained to the day of his death 'the studied pose of infallibility' which he had assumed on his accession. Since he had few personal contacts with his civil service he distrusted them, spent much time checking as far as he could the information they supplied and when they did, greatly daring, offer him advice, he usually showed little inclination to take it. Lack of personal contact was most serious in making senior appointments. On the basis of reports from the presidents of provincial chambers, Frederick often drew up a short list of candidates and then made the appointment after a competitive interview.

The worst fault of the cabinet system as developed by Frederick was its failure to coordinate the central agencies of administration. Frederick refused to delegate this task to the

General Directory. Without depriving it of its nominal superiority, he set up specialized agencies responsible to himself which restricted its effective control of the administration. The earliest of these was entrusted in 1741 with the promotion of trade and industry and became entirely independent of the General Directory in 1769. In 1742 control of the conquered province of Silesia was handed over to another specialized agency.

Frederick also weakened the collegiate basis of the General Directory, i.e. the joint responsibility of its leading officials for all decisions taken by it. He authorized some of its officials to handle certain matters independently of their colleagues and to correspond directly with him. These changes were intended partly to speed up the taking of decisions, partly to relieve Frederick himself of as much routine business as possible without destroying the whole cabinet system. In practice Frederick's changes necessitated a steadily increasing mountain of inter-departmental correspondence, much of which he, as the umpire between the claims of the different departments, had to read.

Only in one direction did Frederick make significant improvements upon the system of centralized government he had inherited from his father. This was in the administration of justice and Frederick personally is entitled to little credit, except that he gave a free hand and when necessary his support to Samuel von Cocceji, the real author of the judicial reforms of this period of the reign. Cocceji had served as Chief Justice in the last years of Frederick William's reign, but had been prevented by the jealousy of his colleagues and the contempt for lawyers, which was a prominent characteristic of Frederick William I, from effecting the changes he had long wished to see in Prussia.

As soon as the second Silesian war ended Cocceji put before the king a sweeping programme of judicial reforms. Frederick accepted in principle though he often violated in practice Cocceji's belief in the independence of the judiciary from the control of the executive. As Frederick himself put it a few years later 'In the law courts the laws must speak and the ruler must remain silent'. This pronouncement has been hailed perhaps rather prematurely as the first step to the creation of the modern *Rechtstaat*—even the ruler is subject to the law. Again Frederick and his chancellor believed that all laws rested on natural equity. Outdated technicalities were abolished. In place of a confused medley of courts with unascertained jurisdictions, Cocceji, before his death in 1755, had established a regular hierarchy of tribunals from local courts of first instance through provincial appeal courts, one for each province, to the newly established High Court at Berlin. The procedure of all these courts was now determined by a code, not by local tradition and individual caprice of the judges. By providing adequate salaries, instead of expecting the judges to live on fees from litigants, and by introducing a system of apprenticeship for judges, Cocceji greatly raised the standard of the judicature.

Cocceji wished also to end the practice by which a government department responsible for administering a law tried persons accused of breaking the law. Likewise he failed, in spite of years of labour, to reduce the local laws and customs prevalent in the various provinces of Prussia to a single law code. This was accomplished in 1795, shortly after the death of Frederick, but the author of this code made little use of the labours of his predecessor. Frederick had written of his chancellor's work in 1752 'One thing is certain. Injustice in the courts has become comparatively rare, the judges are less corrupt, trials shorter and there are fewer cases pending.' Coming from a sovereign who treated his ministers as Frederick habitually did, this is praise indeed.

Frederick approved of the reforms because he believed that they consolidated and strengthened the Prussian state: Cocceji and later jurists laid emphasis rather on the better security they afforded to the property rights of the citizen.[1] Except in judicial matters, such changes as Frederick made were mainly at the top level of

---

[1] See Herman Weil, *Frederick the Great and Samuel von Cocceji* (Madison, Wisconsin, 1961).

government. The local authorities, especially the chambers, continued to deal with governmental business at provincial level, including taxation, collection of revenues from royal domains, internal colonization, and the development of commerce and industries. They still operated as colleges, but were no longer so closely controlled by the General Directory. Since their functions were expanded and their presidents now corresponded directly with the king, they became 'the most vital centres of the entire bureaucratic mechanism'.[1]

While in 1740 all these functionaries regarded themselves as servants of the king and already formed a special class, Frederick substituted the idea of state service and also increased the stratification of the civil service. Whereas Frederick William had lacked confidence in the provincial nobility and regularly used men from the middle class even in the highest civil service posts, Frederick systematically appointed noblemen to serve both in the central organs of government and in the superior posts in local agencies. The lower posts on the other hand were normally filled by former non-commissioned officers or by ex-privates whose wounds rendered them unfit for further military service. He could count in the main on their loyalty, discipline and efficiency as excise collectors and messengers.

So far as the higher ranks were concerned each

[1] W. L. Dorn in *Political Science Quarterly* XLVII, 83.

central department and provincial chamber had its fiscals, officials whose duties were to act as spies upon their colleagues to make certain that they carried out their duties exactly as prescribed in royal regulations, and to ensure that all financial profits were duly lodged in the royal exchequer. Frederick's much publicized journeys throughout the length and breadth of the kingdom were partly designed to secure the same objects. More effective was the practice by which the king required senior officials to submit each year secret conduct reports on all the civil servants, central and local, in his office.

Under Frederick civil service salaries were adequate though certainly not generous—it was not for nothing that *travailler pour le roi de Prusse* came to be a synonym for working without much reward. Malversation was rare though occasionally civil servants managed to save themselves trouble by short cuts of which their master would have disapproved. Those who were caught by the king were summarily dismissed and sometimes shut up in the state prison at Spandau. The virtues and vices characteristic of Prussian and later German bureaucracy were already firmly established in Prussia under Frederick the Great.

Chapter Six

The Diplomatic Revolution and the Origins of the Seven Years War

FREDERICK'S alliance with France, forced upon him by Austria's refusal to pay his price in 1740–1, survived the strains of the Austrian Succession War and remained in force after the treaty of Aix-la-Chapelle. But there was little confidence and less cordiality between the allies. Frederick had repeatedly deserted France and in his turn Louis XV had deliberately exposed Frederick in 1744–5 to crushing defeat. Louis resented Frederick's insistence that he should be treated as the equal of the king of France. On his side Frederick remarked bitterly that to be the ally of France was to be her slave. Worse still his witticisms at their expense infuriated Madame de Pompadour as well as the king of France. In the years immediately after the end of the Austrian Succession War, aggressive Russian actions in the Baltic, primarily directed against Sweden, alarmed Frederick and made him fear that France would use him as a cat'spaw to reduce pressure on her favoured ally, Sweden.

Meantime Frederick's relations with Britain which had been relatively cordial in 1748 deteriorated rapidly. During the Austrian Succession War the British navy had seized some Prussian merchant ships and the government refused to compensate the owners. Frederick promptly retaliated by stopping payment to British bondholders both of interest and capital of the Silesian loan. Frederick's seizure of East Friesland, to which Hanover also had claims, on the death of the duke in 1744, strengthened George II's chronic sense of grievance against his Hohenzollern relations. Worse still, in an attempt to improve relations with Austria and to avert one likely cause of a general European war, Britain engaged on a scheme to secure the election of Maria Theresa's eldest son, the archduke Joseph, as king of the Romans. If this scheme was to have any chance of success the votes of the German electors would have to be purchased and Britain had to engage on a futile competition with France, which set Germany in uproar. Frederick was so annoyed that he retaliated by pretending to take up the Jacobite cause and by leading the opposition to the election of the king of the Romans. By taking up this scheme Britain had thrown France and Prussia into each other's arms.

Frederick knew well that it would be much

more difficult to gain more territory than it had been to acquire Silesia. His neighbours were on their guard and his rivals were jealous of his success. The domestic troubles which had prevented Russia from taking much part in the Austrian Succession War, and had given him almost complete freedom of action, had been surmounted. Peter the Great's daughter Elizabeth was now securely established on the throne and anxious to revive her father's policy of active intervention in central European politics. For a time Frederick thought he had secured himself by arranging a double marriage. His sister Louise Ulrica married the Crown Prince of Sweden while Elizabeth's heir, Charles Peter of Holstein-Gottorp, married Sophia of Anhalt-Zerbst, daughter of a Prussian officer and protégée of Frederick.

Soon the Tsaritsa escaped from Frederick's clutches. What Frederick regarded as harmless jests about her private life transformed her into his personal enemy. She came increasingly under the influence of her chancellor, Alexis Bestuzhev, who believed that hostility between the two rising powers of north-eastern Europe was inevitable. Strengthened by the acquisition of Silesia and the personal reputation of the young king, Prussia now occupied the place of Sweden under Charles XII. Before Russia could safely resume the policy of westward expansion associated with Peter the Great, she must crush this new rival power.

Russia already had a recent tradition of alliance with Austria and the two powers in 1746 made common cause against Prussia in the treaty of the two empresses. If Frederick broke the treaty of Dresden which had ended the second Silesian war, Russia promised to assist Austria with 60,000 men and to continue the war against Prussia until Austria had recovered Silesia and Glatz. Russia's reward would be East Prussia. These projects were known to Frederick, who had his spies well posted. As he himself explained the king of France had twenty cooks and only one spy while he had only one cook and twenty spies. Several of these operated successfully at Dresden, the capital of Saxony and now through its Polish connexions a Russian satellite, where Count Brühl's security system badly needed tightening up.

Frederick could see little hope of effective help against the menace of the two empresses. He had rebuffed the British government in 1748 and was now quarrelling bitterly both with Britain and Hanover. He was uneasy in his French alliance, contemptuous of Louis XV and his ministers, afraid that France would gladly involve him in trouble and then leave him to his fate. If Russia's aggressive attitude in the Baltic immediately after the end of the Austrian Succession War was intended to produce this result, Frederick skilfully evaded the trap.

Frederick's incurable optimism shines out from his *Political Testament* of 1752, intended to give good advice to his heir. Though present circumstances were unfavourable, things would change. Largely for strategic reasons the most desirable territorial acquisitions for Prussia would be Saxony and West Prussia. Saxon territory reached to within a short distance of Berlin and made it difficult to defend his capital. West Prussia would link the outlying province of East Prussia firmly to Pomerania and the central core of Brandenburg. It would however be fatal to attempt anything until the political omens were more favourable.

Instead between 1752 and 1755 the outlook for Prussia steadily deteriorated. Britain and France became involved in a colonial and maritime war. When Frederick proposed that France should punish George II by invading Hanover, France replied that she expected Prussia to do her this service and offered Frederick the rich reward of a West Indian island. Britain meantime was being driven step by step into closer association with the two empresses in order to obtain an assurance of Austrian help, particularly in the Netherlands and for the defence of Hanover, against France. Austria replied that she could not do much in western Europe since she was greatly weakened by the loss of Silesia and had two deadly enemies, Frederick and the Turks, on her own doorstep. Under Austrian pressure Britain concluded at St Peters-

burg a treaty of subsidy with Russia for the hire
of Russian troops (August 1755). Even earlier
Russia had been collecting troops and conducting
military manoeuvres in her Baltic provinces. The
treaty with Britain would meet part of the cost and
at the same time give the Tsaritsa a colourable
pretext to build up a formidable force in the
neighbourhood of East Prussia.

Left to themselves Elizabeth and Bestuzhev
would probably have attacked Frederick before
1755: what held them back was the influence of
Maria Theresa's new chancellor, Kaunitz. Unlike
Frederick, who was always expecting some stroke
of good luck, Kaunitz was a chronic pessimist.
Austria was going downhill; her only hope was to
end the centuries' old duel with France, as many
diplomatists had tried to do in the last half-cen-
tury, and, much more difficult, persuade France to
join with Austria and Russia in partitioning the
Prussian state and reducing its upstart king to the
position of a German elector. Curiously enough
he did not believe that the two empresses were
capable of carrying out this programme unaided,
if only because to keep Russian troops in action
large subsidies would be required. In the summer
of 1755 he suspended negotiations with Britain
and made an all-out attempt to win the concur-
rence of France.

When she signed the subsidy treaty with Russia, Britain had no notion of the use to which

Bestuzhev and Kaunitz meant to put it. Newcastle, the minister responsible for British foreign policy from 1744 to 1756, had his own ideas about using it. Instead of waiting until Prussia threatened Hanover and then paying an enormous war subsidy for inevitably dilatory Russian help in its defence, why not leak the gist of the treaty to Frederick and thus persuade or coerce him to remain neutral?

Frederick had at first viewed the approach of hostilities between Britain and France with pleasurable anticipation and he prepared to be courted by both western powers. They could probably be induced to bid against each other for Prussian help, perhaps even for Prussian neutrality. And there was always the glittering prize that if both powers could be induced to accept his mediation he might arrange a peaceful settlement, which would get Prussia out of immediate difficulties and set the seal upon his reputation as the ablest diplomatist in Europe.

The news that Britain, as he saw it, had joined the two empresses by the St Petersburg treaty and would support the attack upon Prussia which Bestuzhev and Kaunitz were notoriously planning so alarmed Frederick that he suddenly concluded the convention of Westminster (January 1756) with Britain. His one ally France showed more and more clearly that, for once, she believed her future lay upon the water and that the last thing she wanted was to be distracted by participation in a continental war. Frederick was ready to humour her by signing with Britain an agreement for the neutralization of Germany, while leaving it open to France to pursue her vendetta with Britain, if she so desired, in the Netherlands. In signing this convention, Frederick made two miscalculations. Believing that Bestuzhev would do anything for money, he erred in thinking British influence at Petersburg was strong enough to prevent a Russian attack upon Prussia. Still worse, he seems to have been genuinely surprised at the violent reaction in France to the Anglo-Prussian convention.

Louis XV was not impressed by Frederick's argument that his temporary *ad hoc* convention with Britain was entirely compatible with his permanent alliance with France; and, even if it were, the way in which Frederick had concluded it with France's bitterest enemy, on his own initiative and without consulting his ally, made it even more insulting than his previous desertions of France. The convention of Westminster so changed the attitude of the French court to the secret negotiations with Austria, which had nearly bogged down at the end of 1755, that in May 1756 Austria and France concluded an agreement closely and deliberately modelled upon the Anglo–Prussian convention—the first treaty of Versailles. Maria Theresa would remain neutral in the

Franco–British war which had now started. Louis XV would not act in any way against the territories of Maria Theresa. But the Franco–Austrian treaty, unlike the Prusso–British convention, included a formal defensive alliance, by which each partner would supply troops or subsidies if the other were attacked in its European possessions.

Frederick had continued to press his interpretation of the convention of Westminster upon France and had indeed convinced the French ambassador at Berlin that he was right. He was annoyed but not at first much alarmed by news of the Versailles treaty. Soon, as the secret negotiations at Versailles continued between France and Austria, he became suspicious and uneasy. Worse still, it soon became clear that British influence at St Petersburg had declined and that the friends of France, backed by the Austrian ambassador, were now in the ascendant. Frederick's spies warned him that the two empresses were about to launch the long projected attack upon Prussia. His hasty signature of the convention of Westminster had extricated Prussia from the frying pan only to land her a few months later in the fire. It must have added to his resentment that he had been completely outmanoeuvred as a diplomatist by his adversary Kaunitz.

What would have been Frederick's best course now it is impossible, even with a historian's hindsight, to say with absolute certainty. He argued that an attack by three Great Powers upon his upstart kingdom was already inevitable. Why let them choose their own time? If he could get his blow in first the coalition might never form. Even if it did, by first conquering Saxony which had proved a thorn in his side in the previous Silesian wars, he could strengthen his defence. It is indeed a criticism of Frederick's statesmanship at this time that he was too much concerned with military arguments and did not give sufficient weight to diplomatic considerations. Also, he was constitutionally unfitted to play a waiting game and too inclined to risk short cuts to his objectives. Disregarding the solemn warnings of his old ally France and the timid expostulations of his new associate, Britain, he marched into Saxony in August 1756. If this was due as Frederick claimed to military necessity, it was a political blunder. By his own reckless action Frederick had created a coalition which otherwise might never have been formed. That he ultimately escaped disaster in the Seven Years War was due to forces he could not have foreseen and still less could control.

Chapter Seven

The Seven Years War 1756–63

THE origins of the Seven Years War produced among German historians a famous battle of books in the late nineteenth century and the embers of the fire still glow. Lehmann contended that under his customary smoke screen of high sounding moral principles and diplomatic man-oeuvring Frederick was once again engaged in an offensive war primarily intended to gain addi-tional, and preferably Saxon, territory for Prussia. But by this time the Prussian king had become a German national hero and the great majority of German historians persisted in accepting without substantial qualification Frederick's own account of the origin of the war.

According to Frederick, the war was one of those preventive wars which he had claimed in the *Anti-Machiavel* were morally just and often politically wise. Thrice armed is he who gets his blow in first. A resounding victory, followed by a rapid occupation of the Saxon electorate, might even intimidate his enemies and would certainly enhance his chances of mediating a settlement of the Franco–British war which had given his enemies their opportunity. If he could get to the Dresden archives quickly enough his spies assured him he would find ample proofs of the intentions of the Austro–Russian–Saxon allies to launch a joint attack upon Prussia. Publication of this material would give him the moral support of Europe and especially of the German princes, and might even convince France that she was making a mistake in abandoning her alliance with him.

There are even some indications that at a time when most men would have been intent solely on saving what they could from the wreck, Frederick was still hankering, as Lehmann contended, for new acquisitions. The final verdict on responsibility for the continental Seven Years War should probably be that Prussia and Austria—the latter egged on by Russia—were about equally to blame: both were pursuing offensive policies the natural outcome of which was war.

Unfortunately for Frederick his Saxon gamble did not succeed. The Saxon army held out at Pirna long enough to prevent Frederick from striking in the autumn of 1756 at his real objective—Bohemia. And when at last he got to Dresden, he found nothing in the archives to justify his treatment of Saxony. There was abundant evidence of jealousy and hostile feeling against Frederick, but no trace of the agreement which Frederick asserted had been concluded by Austria and Russia, with Saxon connivance, to launch an attack upon him. Militarily he had given Austria warning and ample time to prepare the defence of Bohemia. Politically he had made certain that France would join with his enemies and take a leading part in the war against him.

Indeed by attacking Saxony rather than Austria he had made much easier the cooperation of Russia and France. Both powers were interested in Saxony and inclined to regard it as a client state. While Russia had put the elector on the Polish throne and kept him there, France took seriously her responsibility as a guarantor of the imperial constitution, to protect him in his electorate. Moreover Frederick himself asserted, after the event, what he ought to have taken into account beforehand, that the tears of the elector's daughter, who was the wife of the Dauphin, contributed to the final decision of France to join in the German war.

Even now the coalition was surprisingly slow to form. Not until 1 May 1757 was its keystone, the second treaty of Versailles, concluded between Austria and France. Russia had acceded to the first (defensive) treaty of Versailles in January 1757, and Austria and Russia concluded in the following month a new offensive treaty against Prussia; but there was never an offensive treaty signed by all three main partners in the coalition. The Circles of the Empire had agreed to raise an army against Frederick in January and Sweden joined the coalition in March 1757.

The total population of Prussia was only four and a half millions, dispersed in detached territories from the Rhine to the Niemen. Frederick would have to fight on at least three main fronts against the converging armies of three Great Powers, each at least a match for Prussia. It is true he had the advantage of moving on interior lines and, so long as he had sufficient troops capable of rapid marching and skilful manoeuvring, he could hope to beat his enemies individually and prevent them from joining forces against him.

The campaign of 1757 began badly for Frederick and finished in a blaze of glory. His invasion of Bohemia proved an expensive fiasco. Though he won a bloody battle under the walls of Prague, Daun defeated him in an even bloodier battle at Kolin. A British–Hanoverian army under the duke of Cumberland, which had operated against the French in western Germany, capitulated at Klosterseven (September 1757). The Austrians recovered most of Bohemia and Silesia and even raided Berlin, while the Russians were occupying East Prussia. Had Frederick been killed by a stray bullet at this stage in his career no one would now refer to him as Frederick the Great. It would have seemed that he had frittered away his life. Beginning as a reforming king, he had retained his father's system and owed to his inheritance whatever he had accomplished. Even as a general he would not have been rated above the Old Dessauer or his own Marshal Schwerin, the victor of Mollwitz. And his death would have been followed not only by the loss of Silesia, but by the devastation of his hereditary dominions and their partition amongst the enemies whose hostility he had provoked by his greed and ambition.

At the very end of the campaign of 1757 came what were probably the two most important of all Frederick's battles. At Rossbach (November 1757) he routed a French army supported by the army of the Circles and at Leuthen (December 1757) he overwhelmed the Austrians by using what soon became his favourite tactic—the oblique order of battle. This consisted of a heavily concentrated attack by first-class troops, adequately supported by cavalry and artillery, upon one flank of a numerically superior opponent while Frederick treated the other wing of the Prussian army as a reserve. If the flank attack succeeded, the rest of the army could be thrown in as required to transform a local success into a complete victory; if not, it was always available to cover Frederick's retreat. The oblique battle order depended for success on the speed and violence with which it was executed: the enemy must not be given long enough to reform and bring his superior forces to bear at the point selected by Frederick. The timing of these

battles was important since they came at the very
end of the campaigning season. No eighteenth-
century army could continue fighting through the
winter and spring months, so Frederick was
assured of a breathing space.

Rossbach and Leuthen saved Prussia from
immediate destruction and determined the shape
of the Seven Years War as a war of attrition. And
what enabled Prussia to hold out in the following
campaigns was not merely the demonic energy and
ability of Frederick himself and his ruthless seizure
and exploitation of every available resource, but
the fact that after the battle of Rossbach Frederick
himself never met a French army in battle. William
Pitt took over the conduct of the maritime war and
decided that Canada could be won on the banks
of the Elbe. The convention of Klosterseven was
repudiated (November 1757) and Prusso-British
relations placed on a sound footing by the con-
clusion of the first of several annual subsidy
treaties (April 1758).

Earlier Frederick had haughtily declined to
accept a subsidy from Britain: now he realized
that without British financial help he could not
hope to continue the war. But in addition to the
subsidy of £670,000 a year paid directly to
Frederick, Britain undertook responsibility for the
conduct of the war against France in western
Germany at a cost which rose steadily as the war
went on. Frederick's flank was thus protected by

his ally Britain, which organized a mixed force of Hanoverian, Hessian, Brunswickian and other mercenaries, to which had to be added a steadily increasing proportion of British-born troops—the whole commanded by Ferdinand of Brunswick, brother of Frederick's unfortunate Queen. Over and over again Frederick was to write in his letters to correspondents that if the French once reached Magdeburg he was finished, but thanks to Britain and Ferdinand of Brunswick they never did. There was no formal treaty of alliance between Britain and Prussia, but successive subsidy treaties contained a clause binding them not to negotiate separately with the enemy.

In spite of its technical imperfections the alliance of Britain with Prussia proved much more popular than Britain's previous alliance with Austria had ever been. Whereas Maria Theresa had been burned in effigy in the streets of London during the Austrian Succession War, Frederick the Great soon became a popular hero amongst all classes of Englishmen. Pubs were called after him as well as after the commander of the British troops who fought in the German war, the marquess of Granby. Beer mugs and tea-pots were embellished with his portrait. One enthusiastic Whig lady, impatient at the delay in negotiating the first treaty of subsidy, sent him a personal contribution of £1,000 towards the upkeep of his army. His Prussian Majesty characteristically spent part of this windfall on the purchase of a flute.

The Methodist leader Whitfield held a special service of thanksgiving for Frederick's victories at Rossbach and Leuthen, while Frederick's birthday was celebrated by the illumination of houses and shops in London and Westminster. Much of this enthusiasm was religious rather than political: evangelicals and nonconformists rejoiced to have as Britain's ally a sovereign who could be represented as a Protestant hero battling against the papist powers of France and Austria. They conveniently overlooked the anomalous fact that the Protestant Swedes were fighting on the Papist side while the Protestant Dutch refused to take any part in the struggle.

The novel feature of the campaign of 1758 was effective and massive Russian intervention. Not only did the Russians continue to occupy East Prussia which they meant to keep after the war and which Frederick could do nothing to defend. One Russian army cooperated with the Swedes in Pomerania which had been promised to the Swedes as their share of the spoil; another attacked Brandenburg itself only to be defeated by Frederick at Zorndorf (August). Though the Russians then slowly retreated to Poland for the winter, Frederick had lost nearly as heavily as the Russians in the battle and whereas the Russians had unlimited reserves, trained Prussian troops

were already becoming scarce. To make matters
worse, in trying to manoeuvre his chief Austrian
antagonist, Daun, out of Silesia Frederick lost the
battle of Hochkirch (October).

In 1759 for the first time Frederick was too weak
to take the offensive and waited for his opponents
to move first. Daun never moved if he could help
it, so once again the Russians took the lead. A new
Russian general, Saltykov, advanced into Brandenburg and after being joined by some Austrian
troops crushed Frederick's main army at Kunersdorf (August). Frederick at first thought all was
lost—he wrote to one of his correspondents that
he was preparing to die like a king. But Saltykov
disagreed with the Austrians over the next move
and finally retired from Brandenburg. Even so,
Kunersdorf, followed as it soon was by the capitu-
lation of one of Frederick's favourite generals,
Finck, at Maxen, lost the Prussians control of
most of Saxony which they had hitherto been able
to use for recruiting men and supplies. The only
bright spot was Ferdinand of Brunswick's great
victory at Minden (August) which checked a
determined French threat to western Germany. It
is a clear indication of the depths to which
Frederick had sunk that, in spite of his firmly held
belief that only the Prussian nobility were sufficiently imbued with a sense of honour to make
them good officers, he was now reduced to giving
many commissions to men from the middle

classes. After the war was over he imitated his
father by removing such officers from the regimental rolls.

By this time most people on both sides were
weary of the war on the Continent. In particular
it had never been popular in France, where it was
felt that the second treaty of Versailles was much
too favourable to Austria. If France was to have
any chance of success in her maritime war with
Britain she must reduce her obligations which
were to maintain an army of 105,000 men in
Germany, along with 10,000 German mercenaries,
and to pay Austria a large annual subsidy, part of
which was passed on to Russia, which could not
otherwise have played much part in the war.

Even Bernis, who had negotiated this treaty,
soon realized that its terms could not be justified;
and when Choiseul became French foreign minister he arranged with Austria the third treaty of
Versailles (March 1759). French military and
financial obligations were much reduced and
France expressly renounced cooperation with
Austria and Russia to recover Silesia from Prussia.
French armies would continue the war in western
Germany and if Britain could be knocked out of
the war by Choiseul's projected invasion, it would
be easy for Austria and Russia, by their own
exertions, to recover Silesia. French disinterest in
the recovery of Silesia forced Maria Theresa
closer to Russia. In March 1760 she formally

promised that Russia should retain East Prussia at the end of the war on the one condition that she herself should previously have recovered Silesia and Glatz.

Though Frederick won notable victories over the Austrians at Liegnitz and Torgau in 1760, by this time the war had become mainly a war of sieges. At the beginning of 1762 the doom which he had so long and so skilfully staved off stared Frederick in the face. Unless the Turks could be induced to attack Russia and Austria, he saw no prospect but utter ruin. The forced resignation in October 1761 of his staunch ally Pitt, and the growing feeling in Britain that continued intervention of British armies in a bloody and expensive continental war no longer served essential British interests, cast doubt on the continuance of British military support, perhaps even of British subsidies. Even Pitt, shortly before his fall, had hinted to Frederick that he might be well advised to buy peace by small sacrifices.

Pitt's resignation had made Frederick suspicious of his ally and he failed to appreciate that Newcastle and his friends in the Ministry were just as determined as Pitt had been to continue the German war until a favourable peace with France had actually been signed. Bute, the favourite minister of the young King George III, on the other hand, quite openly avowed his feeling that Frederick was demanding too much of Britain. He

was ready to continue paying a subsidy to
Frederick but wished to end at the earliest possible
moment the active participation of British troops
in the German war.

Since these troops were fighting against France
a separate peace with France would enable Bute
to withdraw them while continuing to subsidize
Frederick to carry on his war against Austria and
Russia. But the treaties of subsidy between Britain
and Prussia, which had been made annually since
1758, contained a clause which bound them not
to negotiate with France except in consultation
with each other and above all not to conclude a
separate peace with her. Frederick in fact did not
object to a separate peace between Britain and
France provided that it secured two things, (1) the
continued payment of his subsidy and (2) the
restoration to Prussia of the Prussian duchies which
had been occupied by French forces in western
Germany.

Meantime the British declaration of war against
Spain (January 1762), with the consequent expansion of the area of colonial warfare and the need
to protect Portugal against Spain, made Bute
more eager than ever to reduce the expense of the
war on the Continent to Britain. Newcastle,
doubting he could resist Bute's wishes much
longer, and determined to maintain in one way
or another Britain's connexion with the Continent,
hinted to Austria that he would like to see the

restoration of the old alliance between Britain and Austria. As an inducement to Austria he proposed to 'come to some regulation with regard to Silesia as should be satisfactory to them'.[1] Kaunitz received the message in a somewhat garbled form and it finally reached Frederick as a convincing story that the British government was not merely anxious to return to the old alliance with Austria, but was ready to purchase its restoration by betraying the vital interests of its present ally.

Bute, unaware of what Newcastle had done, then told Frederick he had better make peace with Austria on the best terms he could get and demanded to know, as a condition of the grant of a subsidy for another year, what were Frederick's plans and resources for carrying on the continental war. Frederick deliberately and quite reasonably declined to reveal these to a power which he now considered capable of divulging them to his enemies. It was the death of the Tsaritsa Elizabeth which enabled Frederick to adopt this attitude. The new Tsar Peter III was far more German than Russian in upbringing and outlook. He had long regarded Frederick as a hero and sought to copy him. He at once declared his intention of making peace with Prussia and restoring East Prussia to Frederick. His fervent ambition was to recover from Denmark his ancestral lands in Schleswig

---

[1] Quoted by W. L. Dorn, 'Frederick the Great and Lord Bute' in *Journal of Modern History*, I, 536.

and Holstein. Frederick offered his support and was soon egging Peter on to attack Denmark. He was careful to conceal this negotiation from Britain, arguing that if Newcastle and Bute were negotiating separately with Austria, he was entitled to negotiate separately with Russia.

What finally impelled him along this course was the communication to him by Peter III of a dispatch from the Russian ambassador at London, Prince Galitzin. Bute, according to Galitzin's report of a conversation with him, had expressed the hope that Peter III would not withdraw his troops from Prussian soil since this would merely prolong the war which the British government hoped to end by exerting pressure upon Prussia to force her to make substantial concessions to her enemies. W. L. Dorn has shown that Galitzin must either have misunderstaood Bute or deliberately misrepresented his views.[1] Frederick reasonably but wrongly assumed that the Galitzin letter faithfully represented Bute's attitude and ordered his envoys at London to break off their negotiation for the renewal of the subsidy treaty with Britain. He made no attempt to discover whether Bute really held the views attributed to him by Galitzin.

Frederick now entered enthusiastically into Peter III's plans for a war against Denmark and thus convinced Bute, who was still ready to pay a

[1] In *Journal of Modern History*, I, 529–60.

subsidy to Prussia to enable Frederick to carry on
the war in Germany against Austria, that to grant
the subsidy would be to give Frederick the means
of attacking a neutral power friendly to Britain.
Under the conditions of 1762 the only justification
for continuing the subsidy was to help Britain to
make a favourable peace with France. Bute had
no intention of paying Frederick to extend the
sphere of operations on the Continent by attacking Denmark. Frederick refused to accept the conditions Bute tried to attach to the giving of the
subsidy and even tried to drive Bute from office by
conducting a newspaper and pamphlet campaign
against him in England. He accused Bute of
deliberately setting out to ruin him, wrote off the
British alliance and placed his reliance on the
Russian Tsar. Fortunately for Frederick, before
he had become too far involved in Peter III's
schemes Peter was deposed and succeeded by his
German wife, who took the title of Catherine II
and refused to re-enter the war. The Swedes, who
had given a remarkable display of military ineptitude throughout the war, now restored Pomerania
to Prussia and withdrew from the coalition (May
1762).

Even Maria Theresa, whose best friends never
claimed that she was over intelligent, saw that
what she had failed to do at the head of a European coalition she could not hope to achieve
unaided. Silesia had finally escaped her clutches.

The treaty of Hubertusburg (February 1763), which ended the Austro–Prussian war, simply restored the *status quo ante bellum*. Frederick even escaped paying compensation to the Wettins for his brutal oppression of their electorate throughout the war. A few days earlier Britain and France had made their own peace of Paris.

Eighteenth-century continental statesmen, notably Frederick, propagated the legend of 'perfidious Albion' by attributing to the British government much higher standards of behaviour than those they knew to exist amongst themselves. Anyhow if Britain had broken her pledge by negotiating separately with Austria, Frederick had engaged much further with Russia and was pursuing a separate negotiation to secure objects objectionable to his British ally. While Frederick was still prepared to continue the struggle and transform it into a war of revenge against Austria, Britain had already secured her objects and was determined to end the war.

Had Bute been less ham-handed and more master in his own house or had Frederick been less suspicious and impulsive, the Prusso–British alliance which had won the war might well have survived into the years of peace after 1763. This would have had important consequences for all Europe. The centre of gravity in European politics would not then have moved so decisively toward eastern Europe. In view of her antecedents and objectives Catherine II would probably have joined a Prusso–British alliance which would have been strong enough to balance the ill-compacted alliance of Bourbon with Hapsburg. It was the attitude of Prussia which more than once contributed to the failure of British attempts to make an alliance with Russia after 1763. Frederick would not tolerate Britain as a third in the alliance he concluded with Russia in 1764. Even after he lost the Russian alliance in 1780 he preferred the dangers of isolation to an *entente* with Britain. Not until after his death did Britain and Prussia come together again. Frederick had not been able to overthrow Bute, but he visited Bute's venial sins upon his successors in office by virtually excluding Britain from participation in European affairs for a quarter of a century.

The mere survival of Prussia is the truest measure of Frederick's greatness both as soldier and statesman. While Frederick had little claim to originality as a strategist and inherited from his father both the formations and system of manoeuvre of his army, he contrived to operate them offensively. He anticipated the basic Napoleonic idea of strategy—the object of all his campaigns, at least until the war of attrition deprived him of the possibility of offence, was not to occupy or hold territory but to seek and destroy the main forces of the enemy, preferably on enemy territory.

But Frederick had to adapt his theoretical ideas

on strategy to the actual situation in which he found himself and to regard him even as the forerunner of Napoleon is really misleading. Napoleon gradually developed and gathered into his own hands overwhelming military resources backed by limitless prestige. Frederick's army was continually fighting against superior numbers whose commanders were convinced that the Prussians must in the end succumb. His victories, important and indeed essential as they were, could never be decisive either militarily or politically whereas a Napoleonic victory would be followed by French occupation of the enemy's capital and his political submission to Napoleon. The best-known Prussian historian of the art of war in the eighteenth century remarked that many of Frederick's battles were no more than a glorified kind of manoeuvring and as the war went on he was reduced to a strategy of exhaustion.[1] Frederick's claim to greatness as a soldier is not affected by such criticisms. He found a middle-way between the Daun-like war of manoeuvre which his brother Prince Henry was always trying to force upon him and the reckless offensives which had ruined Charles XII of Sweden in a previous generation.

Frederick himself, after the Seven Years War was over, was inclined to think he had overdone the offensive approach to war and argued in

[1] Quoted by W. L. Dorn, *Competition for Empire*, pp. 330–1 (New York, 1940).

favour of a war of position. In 1768 he wrote that 'to win a battle means to compel your opponent to yield you his position'.[1] Immediately the war was over he set about strengthening his fortresses and building new ones at strategic points. Even in old age he still believed in offensive tactics, if not in offensive strategy, and emphasized particularly the element of surprise to which he himself owed many of his victories. As a soldier, he 'embodied the utmost in military achievement that was possible in Europe in the conditions prevailing before the French Revolution'.[2]

Whatever may be said about the statesmanship which had involved Prussia in the war, once in, Frederick showed as a statesman much the same qualities as he had done throughout the war as a soldier. He sought to break up the coalition by detaching France, but without success. He managed to secure from Britain much more effective support on the Continent than Austria had ever done in the preceding war of the Austrian succession. He began to take an interest in the Eastern Question and even vainly hoped for Turkish cooperation against Russia and Austria. He jumped unhesitatingly at the Russian alliance when the possibility offered in 1762 even if it meant involving Prussia in a new war in which she might be opposed by Britain, as well as Austria

---

[1] *New Cambridge Modern History*, VII, 172.
[2] *Ibid.*, 171–2.

and France. Frederick's enterprise is as remarkable as his constant attention to the detail of
diplomacy and negotiations when most men
would have been fully occupied with the military
aspect of the war. His greatest advantage was the
combination in his own person of supreme military
and political authority.

No other eighteenth-century ruler could have
done what Frederick had done; but survival was
at the cost of almost all that makes life worth
living. One-ninth of his subjects had perished and
most of his provinces had been repeatedly devas-
tated as the armies of friend and foe marched
and countermarched across them for seven years.
Only East Prussia, securely held by the Russians
from 1758, had escaped comparatively lightly.
Frederick compared the condition of his kingdom
in 1763 to that of Brandenburg when his ancestor
the Great Elector came to power towards the end
of the Thirty Years War. Worse than the economic
disaster was the decline in morale. Even the civil
service in Frederick's view was no longer efficient
and impartial and all classes were looking after
their own interests without regard to the common
weal.

It should be added that Frederick was certainly
exaggerating both the material and moral damage
suffered by his kingdom during the war. He still
possessed enormous war magazines which could be
used to restore agricultural production to peace-

time levels. And by debasing the coinage, saving on British subsidies, and squeezing Saxony and Bohemia dry, he had accumulated sufficient ready money to fight another two campaigns. The war chest was used to restart the whole Prussian economy and heavy taxation of the restored agriculture, industries and commerce enabled him to replenish and even increase his cash resources.

The war had left its mark on the ruler as well as on his kingdom. When he returned to Berlin he told his sister, the queen of Sweden, that he felt a stranger in his own capital. The buildings were the same, but the old friends were dead or scattered. And the Berliners who had known the king before the war would hardly have recognized him now, with his grey hair, bent figure, impaired digestion and permanently embittered outlook on life. Even so, he was well aware that as long as he lived Silesia was safe and Prussia would be treated by his contemporaries as a Great Power.

Chapter Eight

Post-war Reconstruction

THE Prussian army in the Seven Years War had saved the Prussian state, which indeed had been called into existence by Frederick William I to support that army. The enormous prestige of the army after 1763 made any thorough-going reconstruction of the Prussian state or of Prussian society impossible. Without military discipline and civilian regimentation Prussia could not have survived. And after the war 'the Prussian bureaucracy contrived to produce, on the economic resources of what was then the least prosperous section of Germany, a public revenue which was greater than that of Russia on the accession of Catherine II, with a *per capita* burden of taxation no greater than that of Austria and considerably less than that of France'.[1]

The rights of the officer corps based on feudal superiority and hereditary serfdom were hallowed by Prussia's success and could not be touched, or even attacked, as long as Frederick lived and Prussian military success continued. The battle of

[1] Gustav Schmoller, quoted by W. L. Dorn in *Political Science Quarterly* XLVI, 404.

Rossbach is often said to have ruined the house of Bourbon: it would be equally true to say that by setting the seal of victory on an artificial creation in Prussia it brought about the disasters Prussia was to suffer in the Revolutionary and Napoleonic wars.

Frederick had no conception of these truths. Even before the war he had been infuriated when a British diplomatist at Berlin had dared to remark that he would rather be a monkey in the island of Borneo than a subject of his Prussian Majesty. Frederick's whole internal system of government and society, as Rousseau pointed out, denied the middle and lower classes any chance of political education. Therefore it should not be regarded as a step in the direction of civil liberty and constitutional government. What Frederick was deliberately seeking to create, at least in the second half of his reign, was an authoritarian bulwark against the liberal ideas that were slowly gaining ground in western Europe. Especially in the eastern half of his dominions Frederick's civil service offered a worth while career to the many nobles whose lands were not wealthy enough to support them and at the same time strengthened their control over their serfs. Alike in east and west Germany the personal interests of noble administrators thwarted the more enlightened views of the king himself on agrarian reforms and better use of land by enclosure.

As Frederick aged the pseudo-liberal reformer

was transformed into a die-hard Tory. Even when supporting Voltaire in his campaign to *écraser l'infâme* he asked whether it was necessary to make a frontal attack on prejudices which had been consecrated by time and urged that it was the duty of all citizens to obey the law even if it was contrary to the dictates of Reason.

The basic decision which Frederick had to take in 1763 was whether to reduce his army or to maintain it at war-time strength in anticipation of further attacks or in readiness for further conquests. The Great Elector as soon as the Northern War ended by the treaty of Oliva, and again in 1679 at the end of the Franco–Swedish war, had at once reduced his forces to a peace-time footing. It was Frederick and his father who started an armaments race: a reduction of the Prussian army even to its 1740 strength would have relaxed international tension. Instead Frederick kept up a peace-time army of 150,000 men and built new fortresses. Yet he was in no danger from France and Britain, still intent on ruining each other, and only languidly concerned in the politics of eastern Europe. Austria was only less exhausted than Prussia: Maria Theresa was at last convinced she must let Silesia go and concentrate on her remaining provinces. Poland was powerless either for good or evil. Frederick had drawn closer to Turkey during the war and hoped to make the Turks serve his schemes.

The only serious and immediate danger which threatened Prussia was the restlessness of Russia under Catherine II. Russia was the only Great Power which had emerged from the war with unimpaired resources and an enhanced reputation, but Catherine readily accepted the hand of friendship which Frederick hastened to offer. A less apprehensive statesman than Frederick, or perhaps we might rather say one with a clearer conscience, could reasonably have risked making a substantial reduction in his military establishment in 1764. Frederick's refusal to run what he regarded as an unwarrantable risk contributed only less than his father's original building up of the Prussian army to set the seal of militarism upon the Prussian state. By the date of his death the tradition was probably too firmly established to be overthrown—unless an even greater king than Frederick the Great had been vouchsafed to the Hohenzollerns.

To avoid bankruptcy some temporary reductions had to be made—most of the 'free batallions' were disbanded. Middle-class officers were dismissed and their places often taken by foreign mercenaries of noble birth. Inspectors of cavalry and infantry were appointed for each province and the regimental colonels subjected to their supervision. Instead of paying to the captains the wages of all the men on the muster-rolls of their companies throughout the year, although many of the soldiers were on furlough for more than six months at a time, Frederick made it difficult for the captains to recruit sufficient foreign volunteers to keep their companies up to strength and still make a reasonable profit for themselves over the year. These economies, welcome as they were, did not do much to reduce the annual military budget, calculated as it had to be at first in terms of a depreciated currency.

Royal commissioners estimated the losses which his subjects had suffered during the war and Frederick doled out partial compensation to each individual nicely calculated to save him from utter ruin and to enable him to make some contribution to the military budget in later years. Food and forage from surplus army stores were handed over to the peasants in the most distressed areas. Livestock, seed-corn, timber for the rebuilding of their houses were also supplied by the state, supplemented by small money grants or loans. The debased coinage was restored to its pre-war standard at the expense of the holders of the debased coins. A state bank was set up at Berlin in 1765 with its original capital entirely provided by the king.

Colonists, preferably endowed with some working capital of their own, were induced to migrate to Prussia. With their help, new villages were established, marshes were drained and wastelands restored to cultivation or afforested. In the interests of national self-sufficiency, Frederick encouraged the growing of potatoes and made a beginning with sugar-beet cultivation. By the early seventies the potato crop was important enough to avert threatened famine. Frederick's reconstruction of rural Prussia did nothing to improve the legal status of the peasantry, but it did give them some security against starvation.

Frederick was well aware that agriculture and forestry must remain the economic foundation of his state; but, as a convinced mercantilist, he was also eager to develop commerce and industry. The basis of his system was a rigid division between rural areas and towns. As he saw it, the function of commerce was to bring in money from abroad and that of industry was to prevent, as far as possible, money from leaving his own country.[1] By their success in fulfilling these duties the townspeople justified their existence. In 1763 Prussia, apart from a little linen, exported hardly anything except primary products, mainly grain, wool and wood. This had to be altered by prohibitions or protective duties on imports which could be made at home and by state subsidies to and stringent regulation of home manufactures.

During the Seven Years War Frederick had controlled the famous Saxon porcelain factory at Meissen. Although the kilns had been destroyed and the experts had taken refuge at Frankfurt, he

[1] F. Hartung, quoted in *New Cambridge Modern History*, VII, 313.

was soon able to restart production. He would have liked to transfer the factory to Berlin where, shortly before the outbreak of war, a porcelain factory, which made similar but very inferior articles to Meissen, had been established. For a time the Berlin factory ceased production altogether, but in 1761 Frederick arranged with a Prussian financier and war-contractor to restart it. Although the new management now had Saxon expertise behind it, he had to intervene personally to save it from bankruptcy in 1763. By supplying capital and giving the Berlin factory every privilege he could think of Frederick kept it working for the rest of his reign, but it was uphill work. Example being better than precept, he used Berlin porcelain instead of gold or silver plate on his own table and also tried to popularize porcelain snuff-boxes. Snob appeal was reinforced by absolute prohibition of the import of Meissen porcelain into Prussia or even its transit across Prussian territory.

Similar attempts were also made to set up or develop the manufacture of linen, woollen cloth, silks, satins and cottons by subsidies, tariffs and prohibitions. These trades were usually organized on the domestic or handicraft system of production. By 1786 silks and woollen goods were the largest itsems in Prussia's export trade and made a substantial contribution to her favourable trade balance of over three million thalers. Less successful were Frederick's attempts to find a chemical method of treating home-grown tobacco which would make it as palatable as the steadily increasing imports from Virginia in order to reduce the need for foreign exchange. Nor did he succeed in making Emden and Stettin the rivals of Hamburg and Danzig for overseas trade. Indeed these attempts and still more the erection of heavy toll-barriers on his frontiers drove foreign merchants to avoid Prussian territory as far as possible and open up more circuitous but less heavily taxed trade routes. They contributed also to bring about tariff wars with his neighbours, Austria and Saxony. Nor did he succeed in concluding important commercial treaties, although diplomatists who represented other countries often asserted that Prussian ambassadors were glorified commercial travellers.

Frederick did, however, do something to reduce internal barriers to trade between different Prussian provinces and constructed some canals. He often complained that his own subjects lacked initiative and technical skill, and would not exert themselves to support his schemes for the advancement of industry and commerce. Indeed it was vain to expect individual enterprise to flourish under such a stringent system of state control which tended to defeat its own object.

In raising the vast sums required to keep up the army and bureaucracy and promote his economic

schemes, Frederick's fiscal theories were sometimes more modern than one might have expected.
For example, he approved of progressive taxation
i.e. he thought his richer subjects should contribute
to the state a greater proportion of their wealth
than the poorer ones. This was not so much due to
his adoption of liberal economic theories as to his
recognition of the practical needs of his soldiers
who, in peace time, each bought his own rations.
It affords in fact another indication of how the
needs of the Prussian army influenced decisively
the political and economic structure of the state.
Since rye-bread was the staff of life, he reduced
taxation of grain and tried to keep prices steady
by a system of state stores of grain; but he raised
the excise duties on meat, beer and wine.

Each Prussian family had to buy a certain
amount of salt, at a price calculated to produce a
handsome profit to the state, which monopolized
production. Tobacco in 1765 and coffee in 1781
also became state monopolies with prices fixed to
yield a massive profit, if not indeed so high as to
render consumption of these commodities by the
majority of Prussians prohibitive. Inevitably there
was widespread evasion and smuggling: Frederick
sought to counter this by tightening up enforce-
ment and employing spies.

When Frederick's ministers insisted in 1765 that
the yield of taxation could not be improved by the
existing tax-gathering agencies under their con-

trol, Frederick consulted his French friends, D'Alembert and Helvétius. The latter advised him to adopt the French system of farming out the collection of indirect taxes to contractors; but in the end Frederick set up in 1766 a new state department, the *Régie*, controlled by a group of French tax-experts and partly staffed by Frenchmen in its lower ranks. The chief officials were paid nearly four times the salaries paid to Prussian civil servants of similar rank. In addition they were to receive a bonus of 5 per cent on any increase in the net yield of the excise which they collected. For a short time the post office was also managed by French experts.

These experiments were extremely unpopular and not particularly successful, but Frederick continued to set up specialized agencies which further limited the powers of the General Directory. Separate ministries for Mining (1768) and Forestry (1770) were established. In addition the officials who operated the state bank and the monopolies in tobacco and coffee were made directly responsible to the king. At the same time he so weakened the collegiate character of the General Directory that 'after 1770 common decisions . . . were the exception rather than the rule'.[1] In pursuing his economic policies Frederick was not merely arousing the resentment of his normally docile subjects. He was also undermining the authority

[1] W. L. Dorn in *Political Science Quarterly* XLVII, 81.

of the General Directory, which had been, along with the army, the twin pillars of the state under Frederick William I.

No enlightened despot made any real attempt to educate his subjects and Frederick was no exception. Primary education continued to be the responsibility of the Church, as it had been in his father's day. At the end of the Seven Years War unsuccessful attempts were made to recruit teachers from the veteran N.C.O.'s of Frederick's army. At times teachers apparently combined teaching with tailoring and other even less compatible employments. Zedlitz helped him to carry out some minor reforms in the schools. Frederick had his own views on the changes needed in the universities, but did nothing to give effect to them. It was, however, in his reign that attendance at a Prussian university, usually spent in the study of economics and jurisprudence and followed by some years of apprenticeship and a state examination, became the normal avenue to civil service appointments.

A few months after the end of the Seven Years War Frederick began to build a new palace at Potsdam on which he spent large sums that would have been better spent on other purposes. His motive may have been to impress foreign and especially enemy powers with the idea that his finances were in good shape and thus deter them from attacking him. More probably he was intent on providing employment for Berlin artists and craftsmen and showing in the building and furnishing of another palace what could be done by the industries which he had set his heart on developing within his kingdom. The new palace may have been designed partly as a showroom; but it also reflected Frederick's personal taste and growing conservatism. The style was still rococo but the scale of the building, its heavy colonnades and the mechanical treatment of its façades, deprived it of any claim to charm. Had Frederick maintained a large family and a court similar to that of Louis XIV, it would at least have served utilitarian ends. Sans Souci represented a charming fantasy of the philosopher king and he continued to live there in comfortable squalor; for his bachelor establishment the New Palace remained a white elephant.

Chapter Nine

The Russian Alliance and the First Partition of Poland 1764–76

HISTORIANS have debated whether Frederick was moved more by greed or by the desire for security in the middle 1750's. After 1763 his foreign policy was dominated by considerations of security. Prussia simply could not afford another war and, since everybody knew this, it greatly limited his freedom of diplomatic manoeuvre. Otherwise a state which had so recently proved its power under a ruler with such a tremendous reputation as Frederick, would have been able to exert more influence upon the general affairs of Europe in the 'sixties and 'seventies. On the contrary, so far as Germany was concerned, the dynamic power in these decades, particularly after the ambitious Joseph II had succeeded his father Francis I as Emperor in 1765, was Austria. No one could describe Frederick, prematurely aged as he was by the strain and stress of the Seven Years War, as static; but his activity was mainly 'running on the spot, mark time'.

To keep Prussia in the position to which he had raised her, continuous activity was indeed essential.

This was due largely to the diplomatic situation in which Frederick found himself in 1763, though it must be admitted that his own blunders contributed to it. He himself had often bitterly regretted his light-hearted signature of the convention of Westminster which had cost him the alliance of France. But even after the end of the war France made it abundantly clear to him that she much preferred her existing alliance with a somewhat chastened Austria. Indeed unintentionally France had now secured what she had long vainly tried to attain—a balance of power in Germany. Now that Austria was no longer actively trying to destroy that balance the Austrian alliance accorded well with the interests of France.

Though his alliance with Britain had worked well for a few years, Frederick had always regarded Britain as a less desirable ally than France. Indeed his ostentatious separation of Prussia from Britain at the end of the war may have been partly intended to make himself look more respectable in the eyes of Louis XV. If so the device failed: France did not even send a diplomatic agent to Berlin when peace was restored. Faced with the unwavering hostility of Maria Theresa, determined to make Britain pay for her 'treachery', and failing to make any progress with France, Frederick at the end of the war was completely isolated.

He had good reason to know that this was a dangerous situation from which he must escape at almost any cost. The only worthwhile alliance open to him was with Russia, now ruled by his former protégée, Catherine II. The Tsaritsa was ready to accept him as her ally, provided he would pay her price, which was cooperation in her aggressive policy towards Poland, which had been used as a Russian advanced base during the war and had become accustomed to occupation by Russian troops.

The last thing Frederick really wanted was to see the Russians permanently established in Poland; but he hoped by allying with Russia to be able to influence and perhaps restrain her. He knew he was running risks but calculated that the unknown was less dangerous than the known danger of isolation for Prussia. Also, up to a point, Russia and Prussia had common interests in Poland. Both states were invincibly opposed to any revival of Polish power and therefore wished to maintain its existing constitution as a guarantee for the continuance of internal anarchy. Whereas previous Russian rulers had placed and kept the Wettins on the Polish throne, Catherine II had already decided to support the candidature of a Polish noble at the next election and break off the

Saxon-Polish connexion permanently. Frederick heartily concurred in this policy.

In April 1764 he signed with Catherine a defensive alliance, originally for eight years, but later extended until 1780. They promised to place Stanislas Augustus Poniatowski, nephew of the powerful Czartoryski princes and discarded lover of Catherine II, on the throne of Poland in succession to Augustus II, who had conveniently died in the autumn of 1763. They agreed also to maintain Poland's anarchical constitution and to give protection to the Dissidents, i.e. the religious minorities, both Orthodox and Protestant, who were being persecuted by the dominant Roman Catholics.

The election of Poniatowski—the first point in their Polish programme—was accomplished with considerable ease, thanks to the absence of a really satisfactory opposition candidate and the failure of Austria and France—the powers hostile to Poniatowski—to combine effectively. It was also a help to have 50,000 Russian troops on the frontiers of Poland and ample funds to bribe wavering electors. For once a king of Poland had been elected without a war and Frederick breathed more freely.

The respite was brief. The Czartoryski princes were eager to strengthen the powers of government and to restrict the use of the *liberum veto*, by which any deputy to the Diet could suspend all business by pronouncing the mystic words *nie pozwalam*. Catherine, from Frederick's point of view, was just as tiresome as the Czartoryski. She insisted that the Polish Diet must grant full political and civic rights to the Dissidents. The Czartoryski retorted that this would not be safe until the *liberum veto* had been abolished. In this controversy Frederick rather reluctantly sided with Catherine. Having secured the advantageous alliance with Russia, he was now having to pay part of the price.

Soon anti-Dissident pamphlets written by Bishop Sołtyk and others set Poland ablaze and the Diet refused Catherine's demands. The Russian minister at Warsaw then organized and armed associations of Dissidents and other opponents of the Czartoryski who combined to defend the *liberum veto* and to secure rights for the Dissidents. The formation of such associations, known as confederations, was one of the cherished privileges of the Polish nobility. Counter-confederations were formed and Russian troops had to try to avert civil war by arresting the Polish leaders of resistance in the Diet. Purged of Sołtyk and his friends, the Diet concluded a formal treaty with Russia and Prussia (February 1768), which guaranteed the unreformed Polish constitution and the rights demanded by Catherine for the Dissidents. The open coercion of the Diet and the already traditional hatred of Russia, now caused confederations of nobles, notably the Confederation of Bar, to spring up all over Poland with the avowed object of repudiating the treaty with Russia and Prussia, preserving the Roman Catholic monopoly of power and freeing Poland from Russian military occupation.

Russia found herself with a guerilla war on her hands which would be costly and difficult to suppress. Naturally she expected support from her Prussian ally. Frederick liked even less the fact that civil war in Poland gave Russia's opponents a second chance of intervention against her. The Turks foolishly took the lead by declaring war upon Russia (October 1768) and behind Turkey stood Austria and France. The clearer it became that the Turks were no longer a match for the Russians, the more likely French and Austrian intervention to save Turkey. Such intervention would probably bring about the general European war which Frederick above all feared.

Frederick knew that, in spite of the French minister's threats, Choiseul could not intervene effectively in eastern Europe unless he was supported by Austria. Therefore he devoted his diplomatic talents to convincing Austria that he was just as opposed as she was to the aggrandisement of Russia and even arranged a meeting with Joseph II at which he held out to the young Emperor the prospect of cooperation at some future date and suggested that meantime they should agree to keep war out of Germany. Since the interview took place on Silesian soil at Neisse, it was generally felt that Joseph had publicly abandoned any thoughts of regaining Silesia. Another outcome of the meeting was the attempt of Austria and Prussia to get both the Russians and the Turks to accept their joint mediation.

At first Catherine, being also engaged in a war with the Polish guerillas, did not make much progress against the Turks. Frederick remarked of his ally's campaigns that it was a case of a one-eyed man beating a blind one. This increased her dependence on Frederick who was able to secure the extension of the alliance for a further period of eight years. At the same time when Russia had ended the war in Poland and began to win victories against the Turks, Russian dependence on Prussia increased rather than diminished, since every victory won by Catherine increased the likelihood of Austrian intervention backed by France. Austria forcibly seized the Polish duchy of Zips in the Carpathian mountains (November 1770) claiming that it was still legally part of the kingdom of Hungary, although it had been part of Poland since the fifteenth century. Then she made a treaty with Turkey (July 1771) by which she undertook to expel the Russians from Turkish territory and to negotiate a peace which would preserve the independence and integrity of Poland.

Joseph and Kaunitz had overplayed their hands and Frederick at once called their bluff. By now he had a foot firmly established in each camp and had persuaded the Turks to appeal for joint mediation by Austria and Prussia to settle their war against Russia. The solution was as simple as it was profitable for Prussia. Since Austria and France vetoed the territorial gains to which Russia thought her victories entitled her on the Danube, Russia should give up these claims and compensate herself in eastern Poland. But such Russian accession of strength in eastern Europe constituted a danger to both Austria and Prussia. They in turn must have compensation elsewhere in Poland in order to preserve the existing balance between the Great Powers of eastern Europe.

Some such scheme had occupied Frederick's thoughts for years; he had vainly tried to interest Catherine in it as early as 1769. By January 1771 Catherine was ready to make the sacrifice. She said to Prince Henry of Prussia, Frederick's brother who was then on a visit to St Petersburg, that if Austria could occupy Zips, other interested powers should also occupy parts of Poland. When Frederick still hesitated, Prince Henry returned home and convinced him that it was safe to do so. This is almost the only occasion in the whole of Frederick's reign when a subordinate played a decisive role in determining a major policy decision, though it should be remembered that, after all, it was mostly a matter of timing. Catherine and still more her minister, Panin, would much rather have kept an undivided Poland as an unofficial Russian protectorate, though some of her courtiers had for some years been pressing her to accept the principle of partition.

Everybody at Petersburg realized that if Russia seized a part of Poland, Prussia would have to be paid in kind for her support. It was Frederick who insisted that Austria must be included in the deal and after a protracted struggle converted the court of Vienna from the policy of opposing Russian expansion to the less dangerous and less honourable, but more immediately profitable policy of accepting compensation in Poland. The longer Maria Theresa resisted these insidious proposals, the more influence Frederick could exert at St Petersburg; and he exploited his position as the honest broker between Russia and Austria to increase the share of Poland originally suggested by Catherine for Prussia and to blackmail Russia into promising to restore to Austria's Turkish ally the Danubian provinces conquered by the Russian armies.

Kaunitz thought he saw a chance to recover Silesia or at least to gain territory in the Balkans which would enable Austria to resume the *Drang nach Osten* which she had been forced to abandon under Charles VI. Frederick treated these proposals with contempt: if Austria was to get territory without fighting for it this could only be in Poland. In other words Austria must publicly accept responsibility for the partition. Henceforth Frederick expected that the three eastern courts would be bound to each other by joint participation in the partition and the resulting common interest in the retention of their Polish territories. What he had in mind may be described as an eighteenth-century version of the so-called Holy Alliance and succeeding league of the three emperors, which were to be so prominent a feature in the international relations of the next century.

Russia and Prussia agreed on their shares in February 1772 and in the same month Austria accepted the principle of partition. Finally the shares of the three powers were defined by treaty in August 1772. Russia would annex a huge slice of Lithuania which adjoined her western frontier. Austria claimed a solid block of territory in south-western Poland across the Carpathian mountains from the kingdom of Hungary. These territories would become under Austrian rule the kingdom of Galicia. Lastly Prussia secured as her share West Prussia—a group of provinces which would completely close the gap between East Prussia and the core of her dominions in Brandenburg, but not including Danzig and Thorn, two important trading towns on the Vistula. However, as Prussia would control the mouth of the Vistula, Frederick did not anticipate much trouble in reducing them to submission by economic pressure and if necessary a cold war.

As long as they dared the Poles refused to accept partition; but Russian pressure and threats to devastate the country around Warsaw extorted the formal consent of the Polish king and Diet (September 1773). At the time the partition was a great personal triumph for Frederick. His diplomatic skill and resolute bearing had persuaded both Austria and Russia to accept his policy and subserve his interests. Although her share was the smallest, Prussia certainly gained more than either of her partners. There were substantial German and Protestant elements in West Prussia which would facilitate its thorough incorporation in the Prussian state under the pressure of the Prussian administrators. While West Prussia had some potential economic value, Frederick was more interested in its strategic importance. East Prussia ceased to be a pledge in the hands of Russia for Prussia's good behaviour and became a Prussian outlook tower into eastern Europe. This set the seal upon Prussia's rise to equality with Austria and made it likely that she, rather than Austria, would inherit Poland's historic rôle of protector of central Europe from Russian aggression.

While Maria Theresa deplored her inability to avert partition, her son Joseph II and her minister Kaunitz gloated over their peaceful acquisition of what was undoubtedly the largest, wealthiest and most densely populated share. Though apparently the greatest gainer at the time Austria lost in the long run. Her new territories were difficult both to defend and to assimilate and merely added a new racial group to her polyglot empire.

In considering Russia's acquisitions, the basic consideration is that, unlike Austria and Prussia, she could conceivably have been able to gain in time international recognition for the informal protectorate she had long exercised in Poland. Catherine tried to eat the pear before it was ripe at a time when the international situation favoured Frederick. Her share was large and geographically and ethnographically desirable, but this was poor compensation for abandoning under Prussian and Austrian pressure the much more ambitious schemes of Panin; especially as at the same time she had had to limit her prospective gains from her war against the Turks.

Catherine did, however, gain advantage from a new treaty she was able to conclude with Poland in 1775. Russia now formally guaranteed the integrity of what was left of Poland, took under her especial protection the anarchic Polish constitution which prevented any revival of Polish power, and secured the establishment of a standing council, packed with Russian nominees, without the consent of which no constitutional changes could legally be made by the Polish Diet. Much to

F.G.—5*

Frederick's relief she now abandoned the violent insistence upon equality of rights for Roman Catholics and Dissidents in Poland which had brought about the crisis.

The one thing upon which all contemporaries and later historians agree was that the partition was a transaction which requires a defence. The partitioning powers claimed that the anarchy in Poland had proved to be a danger to the peace of Europe. This had some justification and in the circumstances of the time it may well be that no other solution could have averted a general war on the Eastern Question. On the other hand Russia and Prussia had deliberately prevented the Czartoryski party from strengthening the government and putting down Polish anarchy and it was indeed Russian military intervention which provoked the disturbances of 1767–8 and resulting international crisis. In any case by not dividing up amongst themselves the whole of Poland the partitioning powers destroyed the validity of their argument—the rump state, with its carefully preserved anarchic constitution, was as great a danger to the peace of Europe as the old Poland had been.

Frederick's friend Voltaire rested the case for partition upon quite other grounds. It was a substantial step to the complete destruction of a bigoted and reactionary Roman Catholic and feudal state. The transfer of the Polish peasantry to enlightened despotic monarchies would improve their economic and social conditions.

Later German philosophers and historians added in the nineteenth century quite unhistorical arguments based on the superiority of German culture and the by then accepted dogmas of nationalism, such as von Sybel's contention that the partition freed half a million Germans in West Prussia from a foreign yoke. Frederick would have smiled sourly at anyone who had put the first of these arguments to him. He would have been completely unable to understand the second.

While the terms of the Polish settlement were being adjusted, the young king of Sweden, Gustavus III, urged on by France and believing that his kingdom was almost as liable to be partitioned as Poland, carried through a *coup d'état* (August 1772). Russia was too preoccupied elsewhere to interfere and the result was an appreciable strengthening of the Swedish monarchy and a diminution of Russian influence in Sweden. Frederick II had always been jealous of Russian domination in the Baltic but in renewing his alliance with Russia in 1769 he had bound himself, if the Swedes altered their constitution to give more power to their king, to join with Russia in a war against Sweden. He therefore exerted himself to make Gustavus III voluntarily re-establish the constitution of 1720, but he also represented to his Russian ally that Gustavus III was not in a position to attack her. Russia in the end protested but allowed the new constitution to be established.

The Swedish crisis and the reluctance of her Prussian ally to give her effectual help made Catherine anxious to end her Turkish war. Here again Frederick and France found themselves in sympathy and combined to influence the Turks to refuse the moderate terms offered by Catherine at the Bucharest congress (1772–3). It was not until 1774 that a Russian crossing of the Danube and advance into Bulgaria compelled the Turks to make peace with Russia at Kutchuk-Kainardji (July 1774).

The details of this treaty were of little interest to Prussia at the time, but the important part taken by Prussia for the first time in a crisis on the Eastern Question was an indication both of her expanding sphere of action and of the general recognition of her new status as a Great Power. No Hohenzollern before Frederick had considered that the Eastern Question could conceivably be worth the bones of a Prussian grenadier. It was his forced alliance with Russia which had placed Frederick in this novel and dangerous situation and he breathed a sigh of relief when the treaty of Kutchuk-Kainardji, after six years of continued war and international crisis, restored peace to Europe.

Chapter Ten

Last Years in Foreign Policy
1776–86

WHILE the complicated partition of Poland and settlement of the Eastern crisis in 1774 was probably Frederick's masterpiece as a diplomatist, his skill was soon taxed by fresh problems. He kept a wary eye on the attempts of Britain to suppress the American rebellion, obstructing so far as he could her efforts to raise troops in Germany, refusing to permit British mercenaries to march through his territories, but steering clear of any recognition of the Colonists and refusing either to open his ports to their privateers or to make a commercial treaty with them. Not until Britain had recognized the independence of her former colonies did Frederick in 1785 make a treaty of amity and commerce with the Americans.[1]

Soon his whole attention was given to the Bavarian succession question. Maximilian Joseph of Bavaria died childless in 1777 and was suc-

[1] See M. L. Brown, *American Independence through Prussian Eyes* (Duke U.P., 1959) and H. M. Adams, *Prussian American Relations 1775–1871* (Western Reserve U.P. 1960).

ceeded by a distant and elderly cousin, Charles Theodore, who was already Elector Palatine. While the new elector of Bavaria had no legitimate heirs he was the proud father of several illegitimate children for whom he was anxious to make provision. He at once struck a bargain with Joseph II by which he accepted Austrian claims which would have given Joseph about one-third of the Bavarian electorate.

In anticipation of Austrian demands, Frederick had already secretly promised France that he would resist any attempt by Austria, still France's ally be it noted, to secure territory in Bavaria. Frederick and France now combined to support the claims of Charles Theodore's legitimate successor, the duke of Zweibrücken, to the whole of Bavaria. Joseph II's schemes would not only have upset the territorial balance in southern Germany. Frederick believed that if they were not stopped at once Joseph would be encouraged to press ahead until he had reestablished Austria as the dominant power in Germany.

He therefore combined with the duke of Zweibrücken and his old enemy Saxony, which also had claims to part of the Bavarian inheritance, to wage war against Austria in defence of the imperial constitution and the rights of the princes. Frederick once again took the field but failed to win the expected victories against his old antagonist of the Seven Years War, Laudon. The armies never came to grips, but spent their time trying to live off the enemy's supplies so that the struggle was sometimes referred to as the 'potato war'. Frederick's admirers deny that the ineffectivenesss of the Prussian army was due to his old age and argue that the diplomatic situation was so favourable to him that he had no need to win a decisive victory in the field.

France would give Austria no help in what she regarded as an offensive war, while Prussia received some diplomatic and moral support from Russia. George III also made clear that his sympathies both as king and elector were with Prussia. Austria found herself completely isolated and had to accept the mediation of France and Russia. By the treaty of Teschen (1779) she had to withdraw all her claims upon Bavaria except to the quarter of the Inn, a small district of no particular importance, which Joseph was allowed to keep as a means of saving his face. Prussia's ally Saxony received substantial monetary compensation for giving up her claims.

In an attempt to persuade Frederick not to oppose his designs in Bavaria, Joseph had offered not to resist the reunion to the electorate of Brandenburg of Anspach and Bayreuth, two margraviates in southern Germany which had long been held by junior branches of the house of Hohenzollern. Frederick's sister Wilhelmina had married margrave Frederick of Bayreuth, who

died in 1763 and was succeeded by his uncle,
Frederick Christian. When Frederick Christian
died childless in 1769, Bayreuth reverted to the
margrave of Anspach, Charles Alexander. Although he lived until 1806 the Anspach line was
obviously dying out and, under old family agree-
ments ratified by the emperors, their lands ought
then to be granted afresh to one or more of
Frederick's brothers as secundogenitures i.e.
appanages reserved for younger sons of the reigning house.

Frederick had always intended, when the last
male of the Anspach and Bayreuth lines died, to
annex both territories to Prussia and, quite early
in his reign, he had extorted from his brothers
formal renunciations of their claims. At the time
when Joseph had made proposals about the dis-
posal of the secundogenitures, Frederick at once
pointed out there was no connexion between this
question and the Bavarian succession. His claims
were legal and Joseph's illegal: nevertheless the
treaty of Teschen included a clause by which
Joseph, as Emperor, had to admit Frederick's
claim ultimately to annex the margraviates.

Frederick, by organizing political opposition to
Austria and making a military demonstration
against her, had been victorious on both counts.
But it was in some respects a Pyrrhic victory.
Joseph attributed his failure to lack of French
support and was confirmed in his belief that what

he must have, if he was to succeed in his ambitious projects, was the support of Russia, even if this impaired the French alliance which had been the masterpiece of Maria Theresa and Kaunitz. Frederick, on his side, contrasted the ineptitude of his nominal ally Russia in the crisis with the sagacity of France.

As soon as his mother died (1780), Joseph paid Catherine II a visit. Catherine was not much more satisfied with Prussia as an ally than Louis XV had been: in any case, with the fall of Panin and the rise of Potemkin at the Russian court, Russian ambitions were temporarily moving away from Poland and being directed mainly to the Black Sea area and the exploitation of the possibilities opened up there by the treaty of Kutchuk-Kainardji. Frederick's attempts to bring about a triple alliance of Russia, Prussia and Turkey were singularly ill-timed; and his attempt to curry favour with Catherine by joining her League of Neutrals in May 1781 cut little ice at St Petersburg, although it did lead to a profitable use of the Prussian flag by Dutch vessels which were transferred to the Emden register of shipping. Joseph II also joined the Armed Neutrality and used the port of Ostend as Prussia used Emden. But Joseph, unlike Frederick, was prepared to give Russia support against the Turks; and this was the price demanded by Catherine for the transfer of her alliance from Prussia to Austria. The con-

clusion of the Russo–Austrian alliance was delayed
for a year by ceremonial difficulties. Joseph was
enough of a Hapsburg to boggle at the recognition
of the imperial title, claimed by the Russian
sovereigns since the time of Peter the Great, in a
formal treaty. In the end an exchange of letters by
the two sovereigns solved this problem.

Catherine agreed to support Joseph's ambitions
in western Europe and especially in Germany.
Joseph in exchange would back Russia against the
Turks and Tartars. In each case support was
neither unconditional nor unlimited: it was clearly
understood that Catherine meant to uphold her
rights under the treaty of Teschen as a guarantor
of the imperial constitution and that Joseph's
obligations to Catherine would cease if in the
course of coercing the Turks she intruded upon his
sphere of interests in the Balkans.

This agreement put a great strain on the Austro–
French alliance. It is true that the relations of
France and Russia had markedly improved. In
particular, by organizing the Armed Neutrality
(1780) to set limits to the exercise of British sea-
power during the American Revolutionary War,
Russia had done France a good turn. In spite of
this, the French foreign minister Vergennes continued to follow the traditional policy of France
in eastern Europe and, as far as he could, he supported the Turks against Russia.

The consequent tension between the allies

France and Austria was increased by a marked divergence between them in western Europe. France had long cultivated the 'patriot' party in the United Provinces and was now encouraging them to overthrow the Stadtholderate, which was generally regarded as the bulwark of British influence there. Joseph on the contrary now launched a cold war against the Dutch. He began by destroying what was left of the Barrier fortresses in the Netherlands and expelling their Dutch garrisons. Since the Barrier was designed against France this was naturally approved by Vergennes; but Joseph's further schemes, especially the opening to commerce of the river Scheldt, which alarmed the Dutch 'patriot' burghers, put France in a dilemma.

Frederick in 1781 had lost his one and only ally, Catherine, and felt the loss all the more because she had been seduced by his much younger rival, Joseph II. Intent upon his personal vendetta with George III and contemptuous of Lord North's ignorance of the Continent, he would not have Britain as an ally, although his favourite consideration of political necessity pointed clearly to a Prusso–British alliance. When Fox came to power for a few months and offered a British alliance to Prussia, Frederick stalled and insisted on what he knew was impossible—Russia must be included in the proposed combination from the start.

This reaction was partly due to Frederick's

recollection of how the convention of Westminster
(1756) had been followed by the terrible Seven
Years War. He conveniently forgot that in between these two events came his wanton invasion
of Saxony. Rather than run any risk as an ally of
Britain of a second Seven Years War on the Continent, Frederick now preferred isolation, with all
its dangers, to immediate aggression. He was confirmed in this decision by the growing tension in
the eighties between France and Austria, which
he thought at last offered him a real chance of
regaining the long coveted alliance of France.

Meantime with Russia behind him, Joseph was
gaining ground in Germany. He secured in 1781
the appointment of his brother Maximilian as
successor to the Archbishopric of Cologne with
the prospect of an additional Hapsburg vote in
the electoral college. In 1784 he was able to annex
some detached fragments of the bishopric of
Passau, which formed enclaves in the Austrian
territories. Thus encouraged, in 1785 he reverted
to a favourite Hapsburg scheme to exchange the
distant and unprofitable Austrian Netherlands
for Bavaria. Along with the Netherlands Karl
Theodore would take the title king of Burgundy
and the opening of the Scheldt would restore commercial prosperity to the Netherlands. The
acquisition of Bavaria would compensate Austria
at long last for the loss of Silesia.

Catherine had exploited the Austrian alliance

to annex the Tartar territories of the Crimea and the Kuban on the north of the Black Sea (1783) and was quite ready to back up Joseph's exchange projects. France, on the other hand, had to choose between Joseph and her supporters in the United Provinces and Vergennes opted for the Dutch 'patriots'. This made possible successful Prussian opposition. Frederick organized a league of German princes (July 1785) with the support not only of Saxony and Hanover but of many Roman Catholic potentates, including the head of the Electoral College, the archbishop of Mainz. Faced with virtual unanimity in Germany, Joseph had to abandon his schemes.

Frederick had won his last victory—a bloodless one. The young king of Prussia who had begun by breaking the laws of the empire ended as the champion of the imperial constitution and the leader of the German princes against a law-breaking emperor. He had shown throughout his reign the worthlessness of the imperial title, unsupported by superior force, and the ways in which the old constitutional forms could be exploited in the interests of a rising power.

Chapter Eleven

Death and Transfiguration

(1)

Frederick's Last Days and Death

THE personal routine which Frederick had established on his accession hardly changed. Day by day he toiled at mountains of state papers. Eichel had died in 1766 and Fredersdorff in 1768; but their places were taken by others. Podewils was succeeded as foreign minister by Finckenstein and Finckenstein by Hertzberg. Year after year he visited the provinces, inspecting, inquiring into and censuring the work of his subordinates and uttering dire threats of punishment if there was no improvement before his next visit. Year by year he drilled his troops and trained them in manoeuvres. 'Were I to make shoemakers and tailors into generals, the regiments could not be worse' he used to say. Now that he was universally regarded as the ablest soldier of his generation, invitations to attend the Prussian manoeuvres were coveted by rising generals all over Europe. By adopting Prussian drill, tactics and strategy they hoped to raise their own troops to equality with the Prussian army, now regarded as the most powerful organization for war in the world. Mirabeau recognized its uniqueness in the often-quoted remark that other states had their armies, but only the Prussian army had a state.

Frederick's capacity for friendship had never been great and naturally diminished with age. Even in his youth his friends were subjected to supercilious banter and brutal practical jokes. The few who still lived in Prussia rarely saw the king. One of them assured a French visitor that Frederick had never known true friendship and was indeed incapable of feeling it. In fact Frederick made few new friends to take their places, with the exception of Charles Théophile Guichard, whom he nicknamed Quintus Icilius, after one of Caesar's aide-de-camps. Guichard, like so many of Frederick's intimate circle, came of French Huguenot stock. Another new friend was Andrew Mitchell, who had shared Frederick's hardships in the Seven Years War and represented Great Britain at Berlin until his death in 1771. It is recorded that Frederick shed tears at Mitchell's funeral but tears always came easily to him on appropriate occasions. Almost the last of the old friends with whom Frederick remained on intimate terms was the Scottish Jacobite exile Keith, 'milord maréchal', who continued to live at Potsdam until his death in 1778.

As the circle of his friends narrowed he showed

little inclination to draw closer to his relations, still less to his wife, whom on his return from the Seven Years War he greeted with the words 'Madam has grown fatter'. His three younger brothers never had much place in his life. He was ten years older than the next brother, Augustus William, who was himself eight years senior to the youngest, Ferdinand. Frederick's relationship with them from the time he came to the throne was that of a severe and critical father rather than that of an elder brother. Augustus William shared his elder brother's taste for books and was created Prince of Prussia in 1744. Entrusted with a command in Saxony in 1757, he, or his generals, was completely outmanoeuvred by the Austrians at a time when Frederick himself was in dire straits. Frederick refused to speak to him, dismissed him from his command, and told him that he need never expect another and could take himself off whither he pleased. The unfortunate prince died a year later, apparently not of a broken heart as was said at the time, but as a result of a tumour on the brain. The youngest of the four brothers, Ferdinand, survived the king for many years. Though he fought bravely in subordinate positions during the Seven Years War he was, personally and politically, a nonentity who never attempted to take any part in public life.

The middle brother in age of the royal princes was Henry, who was much the strongest character of the three. He had bitterly criticized his brother's diplomacy during the Diplomatic Revolution and still more his decision to wage a preventive war against Saxony in 1756. Frederick's suspicion that he stirred up the other brothers to oppose their king and would have liked to lead the whole Hohenzollern family by the nose was well-founded. Naturally he took Augustus William's side in the quarrel of 1757 between the king and the prince of Prussia. Indeed he never forgave Frederick as long as he lived; after Frederick's death he erected a monument to the heroes of the Seven Years War which made public his cherished view that Augustus William was the chief of them and that Frederick was not even included amongst them.

During the Seven Years War Prince Henry carried on a personal policy of secret negotiation designed to detach France from the coalition against Prussia, and bitterly criticized as ruinous and insane the offensive strategy and tactics of his brother. His own ideas of strategy were not very different from those of Daun—a cautious defensive campaign was his ideal—and his biographer contends that this made him an invaluable coadjutor of his brother as virtual second-in-command.[1] It was Prince Henry who covered up after his brother had won or lost an offensive battle which,

[1] Chester V. Easum, *Prince Henry of Prussia* (University of Wisconsin Press, Madison, 1942), pp. 57-58.

whatever its outcome, so weakened his own army as to reduce it to temporary inaction. However this may be in retrospect, it certainly did not make cooperation between the brothers easy during the war. Frederick's compliment, if indeed he ever made it, that Henry was the only Prussian general who never made a mistake was patently insincere. Henry did, however, beat the Austrians at Freiberg in 1762, the last important battle in the war and the only major victory won by Prussian troops not under the personal command of the king.

In spite of this achievement Frederick firmly reduced him to his pre-war rank of colonel of an infantry regiment as soon as the war was over. When he was restored to an independent command in the War of the Bavarian Succession, he professed to be more afraid of his brother's mistakes than of the enemy. Indeed he laid the blame for Prussian failure to win a victory over the Austrians in the new war on the despotism of his brother, who had reduced to servitude men who would have responded to the spur of honour. He himself would have preferred to strike a bargain with Joseph II at the expense of the lesser German states and thus avoid the need to fight a campaign at all. When he thought Frederick was going to continue the war for a second campaign he meddled with Frederick's negotiations at Teschen and brought about at last a definitive political breach between himself and the king. Retiring to Rheinsberg he held a court for all the disaffected nobility.

As a diplomatist Henry's one achievement was his contribution to the first partition of Poland. His special missions to France and Sweden produced no tangible benefits for Prussia though the former confirmed his lifelong position as leader of the Francophil party at Berlin. His second mission to Russia in 1776 at most kept alive for a few years the alliance between Russia and Prussia which had already lost and never recovered either its cordiality or its efficiency. But it appears that he himself took the initiative in securing from Catherine II an invitation to visit her in 1770 and early in 1771 the Tsaritsa, in a half-joking conversation with Prince Henry, invited Prussia to occupy part of West Prussia. Prince Henry returned posthaste to Potsdam and spent a week closeted with the king working out the necessary manoeuvres. His biographer believed that in this period 'he overcame the king's hesitation by convincing him that it would be safe as well as profitable to go ahead' and concludes that 'no other of [the king's] servants was ever able to persuade Frederick to reverse himself so completely or so suddenly on a matter of such major importance; and none was ever permitted, even temporarily, so to take the play out of the king's hands'.[1] Apparently it is not

---

[1] Chester V. Easum, *Prince Henry of Prussia* (University of Wisconsin Press, Madison, 1942), pp. 270-1.

suggested that the Tsaritsa's approach was due to her personal esteem for Prince Henry. This being so, it is easy to argue that had Prince Henry not been available she would simply have used another channel to communicate with the king of Prussia. No one who has studied Frederick's statesmanship and his cautious earlier attempts to interest her in a partition of Poland can doubt what his response would have been.

Unlike most childless men, Frederick throughout his life showed little affection for his nephews and nieces, with the solitary exception of Henry, the younger son of Augustus William, a promising Hohenzollern who died in 1767 at the age of nineteen, much lamented by his uncle. The elder brother of the young Prince Henry, Frederick William, soon proved as incompetent as he was untrustworthy. Frederick described him as incorrigible and made only half-hearted attempts to turn his frivolous and dissolute heir into a soldier or a statesman. So convinced was he of the dangers to which the accession of such a feeble prince would expose the Prussian state that he toyed for a time with the idea of making the elder Prince Henry official guardian of their nephew when, on Frederick's death, Frederick William would succeed him on the throne. Either because of the quarrel between Prince Henry and the king at the end of the Bavarian Succession War or because he realized the impossibility of limiting the authority of his

successor after his death the scheme was soon abandoned. In this respect at least Frederick followed the
line of least resistance—after me the deluge.

In his self-imposed seclusion as the hermit of
Sans Souci he no longer found much enjoyment in
reading the fashionable contemporary authors.
The distinguished literary men who had given distinction to the Berlin Academy were dead or gone:
such distinction as it retained was due to the
mathematicians and scientists in whose work he
had never taken more than a superficial interest.
With the exception of Grimm he took a poor view
of the *Encyclopédistes*. He was annoyed by Diderot's
intellectual arrogance and offended by the atheis-
tical dogmatism of Holbach and Helvétius.
D'Alembert was always making idiotic sugges-
tions: why did Frederick not place a bust of Voltaire in the Roman Catholic church at Berlin? He
even protested against Frederick's reception of the
Jesuits exiled from France. As for that poor sim-
pleton Rousseau, his *Emile* was unoriginal and
wearisome.

Nor did he turn from decadent France to the
literature of his own country, slowly gathering
elegance and force, and at least to an extent
nurtured by his own political and military
achievements. In spite of its subject matter,
Lessing's *Minna von Barnhelm*, held by many to be
the best as well as the first of German comedies,
meant nothing to him. Goethe's *Werther* and

Götz von Berlichingen filled him with despair. A writer so influenced by the execrable plays of Shakespeare, who owed nothing to Racine, ignored the dramatic unities and wrote in German, a half-barbarous jargon, was beyond the pale of Frederick's comprehension.

His views on German as a literary language were forcibly expressed in his treatise *De la Littérature Allemande*, published in 1780, in which he advocated the reform of university teaching, and particularly a greater use of the historical method in the study of philosophy and law. So far as history itself was concerned, historians should give more attention to the history of Germany from 1648. Savage as was his attack on German pedantry and literature, he foretold a glorious future for the German language and German literature, if only the princes, each in his own dominions, would become discerning patrons. Why then did he not show the way? When Mirabeau asked Frederick why the Caesar of the Germans was not also their Augustus, he received the reply that Frederick had done German writers the best service in his power by allowing them to go their own way; but this retort can only be described as special pleading. As in literature, so it was with Frederick in music. He still visited the opera and played on the flute the tunes he knew of old: the contemporary music of Haydn and Gluck he despised.

As he grew older Frederick grew steadily shabbier. He wore a threadbare blue coat, its pockets bulging with snuff boxes, scuffed velvet trousers and a large *tricorne* hat. This outfit was completed by a battered old sword. His clothes were invariably stained with snuff. The dandy of a crown prince who had despised his father's economies, had become a miserly old man. The soldier who looked after his wardrobe sewed buttons on his coat with white thread and patched his shirts: Frederick did not care. The guest rooms at Sans Souci, no longer required, were shut up. The furnishings of the rooms he still used became as shabby as his clothes. Like many elderly men he found much pleasure in his meals and developed a taste for highly spiced dishes. Only a few weeks before his death he dined on heavily spiced soup, beef soaked in brandy, a whole plate of eel pie, maize and cheese flavoured with garlic. He still had a fondness for champagne: otherwise he often mixed water with his wine. Wrinkled, emaciated, round-shouldered, leaning on a stick which served sometimes as a crutch, he went about his business—still the first servant of the state and still constantly re-reading, revising and annotating the literary works which he had once hoped would be his passport to the hall of fame.

The stream of literary visitors to Potsdam are almost unanimous that to his dying day, in spite of his slovenly attire and ill-kempt surroundings, the aura of majesty clung to Frederick. It is hard to tell whether they were merely observing a literary convention or had the perception to see the reality beneath superficial appearances. He himself loved to show off to strangers and give once again to a new audience his celebrated impersonation of the philosopher king. His conversation became more and more autobiographical. French visitors never ceased to marvel that a personality who would have been such an ornament to the salons of Paris had been educated and spent all his life in Germany; but usually they had the sense to keep their thoughts to themselves until they had returned to France.

It is hard to tell what his own subjects thought of him. The mass of the peasants owed something to his care of their economic interests, self-interested though it was. The veterans who had fought in the Seven Years War and survived to tell the tale often worshipped him. They would greet him as 'Father' and perhaps call him 'Old Fritz' behind his back. On the other hand his constant carping criticism in the post-war years must have offended many of his officers and civil servants. When he visited Berlin or a provincial capital like Breslau, crowds gathered to watch him pass— some even tried to kiss the skirts of his cloak or lick his worn yellowed boots. Yet according to Mirabeau, who was an eye-witness of what happened at Berlin when Frederick died on 17 August 1786, everyone in the Prussian capital had been wishing for the end of the reign and rejoiced that it had come at last. This was largely due to resentment at his economic policy and particularly the burdens of the excise duties enforced by French officials; but we may well feel that it was just retribution towards a king who, in spite of his lofty professions of devotion to their welfare, had never ceased to regard the mass of his subjects as *canaille* and cannon-fodder. His wish to be buried on the terrace at Sans Souci was set aside. After lying in state at Potsdam for a single day his body was transferred to the vault of the garrison church there. The coffin was then placed by the side of his father's and in death the two enemies were at last reconciled. The debate among the living as to which king had done more for Prussia had already begun.

(2)

Frederick William I and Frederick the Great

Both kings were essential to the greatness of Prussia. Frederick William had forged the weapons—a superb army, an efficient bureaucracy and a docile and industrious people—but did not know how to use them. Frederick would

have achieved as little without them as his father
had done with them. Without his father's army at
his back he could never have challenged the Hapsburgs and have laid violent hands upon Silesia.
This stroke largely determined the whole character of his reign. Without his father's regimentation
of the whole life of his people Frederick could
never have retained and digested Silesia until by
the end of his reign it had been completely incorporated in Prussia. Frederick did not merely
believe, as did his father and most orthodox
mercantilists, that defence was more important
than opulence: he valued prosperity mainly
because it strengthened his defences.

And it was to his father that he owed his absolute
control of the finances and fiscal policies of the
Prussian state, unfettered by the local Estates,
which still retained in some of the middle states of
Germany a right to be consulted in financial
matters, or even continued to operate a separate
financial system of their own, entirely distinct
from the prince's administration. In Prussia the
king had a more direct interest in the economic
welfare of his country. Every increase in the prosperity of his subjects increased in equal proportion
the resources of the Prussian state. Again Frederick
owed to his electoral predecessors and particularly
to his father, who was notorious for his lifelong
efforts to improve his estates—*ein Plus machen*—the
advantage that in Prussia the income derived from

the royal estates was proportionately greater than in the lands of his nearest competitors and particularly in Austria. The royal domains in 1740 'constituted one-fourth of all the land of the Prussian monarchy and yielded one-third of the entire public revenue'.[1]

Nevertheless Frederick's personal contribution to the rise of Prussia is unchallengeable. It was he who eliminated the last traces of local patriotism: henceforth all subjects of the kings of Prussia regarded themselves as Prussians. His achievements as soldier and statesman gave them a feeling of superiority to Saxons, Hanoverians, Bavarians and all the other peoples of the Empire. It was his good fortune that his Hapsburg rivals failed to effect a similar transformation of their estates, which were only less scattered than his own, and much more diverse in political development and cultural affinity. Except for some recently incorporated Poles, all subjects of the Hohenzollern kings were now Prussians, whereas the Hapsburgs still ruled over Germans, Bohemians, Magyars, Poles and South Slavs.

Prussia in Frederick's hands became a state whose centralized efficiency had no parallel in Europe. Contemporary France witnessed a marked revival of the power of the nobles as well as a notable increase in the claims of the bourgeoisie. While many other absolute monarchies existed in

[1] W. L. Dorn in *Political Science Quarterly* XLVII, 77.

eighteenth-century Europe, in none was the reality of absolute power in such close accord with the theory. Though he despised the mass of his people, Frederick was an adept at public relations. The legal reforms of Cocceji early in his reign and the work of Johann von Carmer preparatory to the codification of Prussian law, although this was not completed until 1795, won the applause of European jurists as well as the approval of his own subjects. The literary works, mediocre as they were, which he published in his lifetime and still more his indefatigable correspondence with European scholars and literary men won him many friends and much influence over enlightened circles.

Partly for these reasons it is customary to treat him as the first, if not the greatest, of the enlightened despots. Hartung believes that he was the first monarch who not merely called himself the first servant of the state but actually lived up to his professions throughout his reign.[1] His father had never advanced beyond thinking of the territories he ruled as his own estates and of his subjects as serfs who had to do his bidding. Frederick's approach to the problem of authority was in theory much more sophisticated, if not enlightened, as for example in his statement that he was not the owner but only the administrator of the

[1] Fritz Hartung, *Enlightened Despotism* (Historical Association Pamphlet [G. 36], London, 1957).

Prussian lands, but in practice he differed little from his father. Indeed Dr M. S. Anderson has suggested that it would be 'hard to point to any aspect of his activities which would have been very different if the ideas of the Enlightenment had never existed'.[1]

For example, Frederick's attitude to religion, while in harmony with contemporary 'enlightened' ideas, owed a good deal to Erastianism, and in some respects foreshadowed Marx. By secularizing the state and disestablishing the Church, he boasted that everybody in Prussia was free to go to Heaven in his own way. The best contemporary comment on this was made by Lessing who pointed out that the vaunted freedom of thought and liberty of the press in Prussia meant no more in practice than 'permission to let off as many squibs against religion as one likes'. Similarly it suited him to distinguish between the momentary ruler and the state, so long as the temporary ruler remained the sole judge of the permanent interests of the state.

This differentiation was the indispensable basis for the Frederician doctrines of political necessity and *Staatsräson*. These came to be as characteristic of enlightened despotism as divine right had been of Louis XIV's absolutism. Frederick used them both in domestic administration and more conspicuously in his foreign policy. Within Prussia he

[1] *Europe in the Eighteenth Century* (Longmans, 1961), p. 123.

established a police state in which all the external activities of each citizen were liable to be regulated according to state necessity as interpreted by the sovereign. This feature alone would seem to justify the current criticism of the benevolent despots that despotism was their end and benevolence merely an occasional by-product.

But the more important applications of *Staats-räson* are perhaps Frederick's continual appeals to it as providing a theoretical or even a moral justification for the tergiversations of his foreign policy. Negotiations without arms, he once remarked, were like music without instruments. The candour with which he explained in 1740 his motives in invading Silesia was soon deliberately obscured by the doctrine of political necessity, which proved equally useful in justifying his outrageous treatment of his allies and his chicanery in bringing about the first partition of Poland. By the end of his reign France, Britain and Russia, who had in succession been his allies were just as reluctant as his old enemy Austria to make an alliance with him.

In 1740, when he had reckoned up his assets, he had grasped the basic fact about the European situation—that he could count securely on support either from France or from Britain, the two strongest and most bitterly opposed of the Great Powers. By 1763 he had exhausted this precious capital. No one in France and few people of importance in Britain, except Pitt, cared about the Prussian alliance. Indeed, neither France nor Britain now exerted their former influence in European politics. By 1780 he had, largely by his own fault, lost his grip on Russia and in the last diplomatic crisis of the reign he was reduced willy-nilly to cooperation with the German princes in the *Fürstenbund*. This action, which under new conditions was acclaimed as a stroke of genius by later German historians, was regarded at the time as a confession of failure.

Against all this, it must be admitted that if Frederick had run through the political capital which he had possessed in 1740, he had gained much by diplomacy and war—Silesia and Glatz, East Friesland with the port of Emden, the various territories usually described as West Prussia and the eventual reunion of the Hohenzollern secundogenitures of Anspach and Bayreuth in southern Germany. Geographically, strategically and economically, if not in constitution and administration, the Prussian state had a new look. Though he himself made rather sour jests in his last years about Prussia aping the Great Powers rather than really being a Great Power, his territorial acquisitions and the enhanced standing of Prussia in European politics proved permanent. Indeed they provided the indispensable basis for further advance under circumstances more favourable than those of 1786.

Whether Frederick could have achieved all this without antagonizing the other European powers apart from Austria must remain a doubtful question. He showed as a diplomatist many of the qualities he conspicuously possessed as a general—initiative, careful preparation and an uncanny sense which enabled him sometimes to anticipate the opponent's moves and exploit his weaknesses. In diplomacy as in war his lifelong motto was 'toujours en vedette'. But the speed of his reactions and the violence of his movements were less admirable in the diplomatic than in the military arena. Still worse, there were occasions when his hunches were wrong, especially when he had convinced himself by subtle analysis that the situation would alter and he tried to adapt his policy in advance to a change which had not yet been completed. Probably his sudden decision to sign the convention of Westminister in 1756 was the most conspicuous example of this. He was much readier to admit his mistakes as a soldier than as a diplomatist. And for all his adroit juggling with five balls at the one time, he sometimes allowed personal resentment to influence his policy unduly. Again, such an astute student of international politics should not have allowed himself to make enemies of so many influential persons at the French and Russian courts not so much by inevitable clash of policies as by indiscreet witticisms at their expense. When in his extremity he tried to make up to Madame de Pompadour, he found the door firmly barred against him.

After the emergence of Kaunitz as the chief minister of Maria Theresa, the easy diplomatic triumphs which Frederick had won in the first two Silesian wars were no longer available. Kaunitz undermined Frederick's diplomatic position successfully before organizing a military attack upon him. His success was due to his exploitation of Frederick's mistakes and his sound appreciation of Frederician psychology. But if Kaunitz won the first round in the duel, Frederick won the second. Austrian participation in the first partition of Poland and Kaunitz's forced abandonment of his alliance with Turkey were as great a victory for Frederick's diplomacy as the Diplomatic Revolution and the coalition of three Great Powers had been a diplomatic defeat for him.

Some German historians, especially Meinecke, have argued that it was imperative political necessity that prevented Frederick from developing in practice the political ideas which he theoretically accepted. Prussia was a new, weak Great Power surrounded by jealous and hostile rivals inherently stronger than herself. In this situation it would have been suicidal for Frederick to break up his father's authoritarian system, based on the army, the bureaucracy, the stratification of society and hereditary serfdom.

This attempt at justification does not carry

complete conviction, at least to a non-German reader. We know enough about Frederick's mental processes to feel sure that even had he been as secure throughout his reign from foreign danger as he was from internal revolt he would never have adopted a genuinely radical attitude towards the system of government and society that he had inherited. Whereas Hume and Voltaire took a rosy view of human nature and looked forward to the rapid spread of universal enlightenment, Frederick, never an optimist, became more and more pessimistic as he grew older. He continued to work for the material well-being of his subjects but did hardly anything to educate them. The thought of educating them politically never crossed his mind, though he did have some glimmering of an idea that it was not necessarily easier to rule over an ignorant than over an educated people. He had no need to face the dilemma of the present day—is self government better than good government?

As a young man Frederick had studied the fashionable works on political arithmetic and political economy, but did little to keep up to date with changing economic ideas. He had some acquaintance with the ideas of the Physiocrats, but none with those of Adam Smith. He remained to the end of his life a staunch mercantilist and never advanced towards more liberal ideas of multilateral trade. To reduce the drain on Prussian currency, heavy duties or complete prohibitions were laid upon many imports. The hope that this would lead to increased home manufacture was not always realized. Indeed conflicts of interest developed between home production and the financial needs of the state. Lower duties while increasing revenue would damage infant industries. In spite of ministerial attempts to enlighten him, Frederick never appreciated the fact that the developing commercial and industrial activities of his subjects needed for their further advance a more flexible and sophisticated economic policy. It was not the least of his mistakes that he looked on the promotion of trade and industry as the peculiar contribution of the middle and urban class to the Prussian state.

More important at the time, since they constituted the great mass of his subjects and provided the recruits for Frederick's army, was his treatment of the peasants. The increased efficiency of the bureaucracy enabled him to exercise closer supervision of the serfs on the domain lands. In 1777 he transferred the precarious holdings of his own serfs into hereditary tenures subject to payment of traditional dues and services. Nothing was done for the individual serfs who lived on the estates of the nobles, but to secure a regular and adequate supply of cannon fodder the Junkers were forbidden to encroach upon peasant holdings or add them to their demesnes. Here alone did

Frederick's lifelong aristocratic sympathies yield to the even more clamant necessities of the Prussian war lord.

These and other criticisms of Frederick's economic policy should not blind us to the greatness of his achievements. In 1740 Prussia had been a small and under-developed country, as unimportant economically as it had been politically. By 1786 it was one of the principal agrarian, industrial and commercial states of Europe. For one thing the population of Prussia, mainly owing to Frederick's conquests but also to natural increase and planned immigration, had doubled in Frederick's reign. Agriculture and forestry had been developed and trade and industry fostered, often at the expense of Prussia's neighbours, Austria, Saxony and Poland. Frederick's life-long belief in a planned economy produced some acute difficulties in his life-time but in the long run it transformed Prussia and laid the foundations upon which was to rest the German Industrial Revolution of the next century. Yet it must be admitted that Frederick's economic ideas and policies were in no way original: they were essentially the same as those favoured for example by his father. The much greater results which he achieved were partly due to the wider scale of his operations, but mainly to the thoroughness and consistency with which they were enforced for nearly half a century.

Frederick had done for Prussia everything

which an enlightened despot could reasonably be expected to do. 'Absolutism had completed its task.'[1] For a generation respect for his achievements was so great that it effectively prevented further advance; and even after Jena it restricted the outlook and imposed narrow limitations upon those who saw the need for radical transformation of the Prussian state.

(3)

The Transfiguration of Frederick

The myth of Frederick the Great has become more important than the reality. It is therefore worth while to trace briefly the transformation of the hard-headed, if enlightened, Prussian king, who was disliked in his own life-time by such varied German authors as Wieland, Winckelmann and Lessing into the 'patron saint of Germany', in Lord Rosebery's phrase. Goethe's attitude towards Frederick varied, though in connexion with the Seven Years War he wrote of the king of Prussia as 'he who stands firm while all around him falter'.[2] A few years after Frederick's death,

---

[1] F. Hartung, *Enlightened Despotism* (Historical Association Pamphlet [G. 36], London, 1957).

[2] Quoted by Veit Valentin in *History* XIX, 121.

Schiller refused to undertake what he called the tremendous task of idealizing him.

The German Romantic writers, in their violent reaction against the eighteenth century, criticized the Frederician state because it was not hallowed by the presence of any higher ideals. Arndt denounced Frederick as un-German, if not anti-German, particularly since he entirely lacked the primitive faith and deep mysticism which he and the other Romantics believed to have been characteristic of medieval Germans. Curiously enough, it was the royal disciple of the Romantics, Frederick William IV, who, aided by Ranke and Droysen, transformed the historical Frederick into the prophet of *Kleindeutsche* nationalism. Frederick's lifelong enmity towards Austria was represented as the first stage of a movement designed to exclude Austria altogether from Germany. His League of Princes foreshadowed the North German Confederation of 1866. Ranke and Droysen accomplished the task Schiller had refused to attempt by linking their interpretations of his character and policy with the political controversies of their own day. At the same time they, unlike previous writers on Frederick, made it their business to study and criticize the primary sources for his life and work which were now becoming available.

Ranke thought of him as the exponent of the balance of power who had brought to its highest

point the European state-system. Droysen saw
him in isolation from Europe as the standard-
bearer of Prussian ideals and argued that his
achievements gave Prussia a legal as well as a
moral claim to make a national German state in
her own image. While he was too good a historian
to think of Frederick as a German nationalist, he
argued that Frederick's work had in fact prepared for and contributed to current conceptions
of Germany as a national state. In his view there
was a clear line of development from Frederick to
Bismarck and from the seizure of Silesia to the
Hall of Mirrors at Versailles. Austria's interests
were non-, if not anti-German. Those of Prussia
accorded with those of Germany as had been
proved while Droysen was writing his *History of
Prussian Policy* by the establishment of the Hohenzollern *Reich* in 1871.

One of Droysen's pupils was Koser whose biography of Frederick is still the standard life. Koser
appreciates his hero's achievements in the belief
that they contributed to the second *Reich* which
gave the biographer as he wrote feelings of personal satisfaction and national pride. 'A great
King who was also a great man' summed up his
view of Frederick. He did not hesitate to invoke
the actual political set-up in Germany as a justification for some of the shabbier deeds which
Frederick had done more than a century before.

Carlyle in his laboured defence and, even more

so, Macaulay in his swash-buckling attack upon
Frederick, were both, like their German contemporaries, more interested in the Frederick myth of
their own day and its political and moral implica-
tions than with the historic Frederick, while the
French historians Broglie and Lavisse were largely
concerned to find out what manner of man he was
who had inspired the Germans to expel French influence from Central Europe and set up an Empire
which had overwhelmed Napoleon III and destroyed the military reputation of France at Sedan.

Within Germany, Onno Klopp's *Grossdeutsch*
predilections and resentment at Austria's defeat by
Prussia in 1866 led him to launch a violent attack
upon Frederick. Klopp's works have been used as
an armoury of weapons by later critics: he himself
found it wiser after his outburst to accept an
appointment at Vienna. Nearly thirty years later
Max Lehmann ventured another attack on
Frederick, but on a much narrower front. He
denounced Frederick's invasion of Saxony in 1756
as the beginning of an offensive war, but hardly
dented the orthodox view that Frederick was
acting in self-defence.

The collapse in 1918 of the Hohenzollern *Reich*,
amid military disasters unparalleled since Jena,
actually strengthened the Frederician myth and
gave it even wider currency. Kaiser Wilhelm II
disappeared into limbo, and there was a slump
in the historical stock of Bismarck, the self-pro-

claimed architect of that empire. Reduced competition raised Frederick's reputation, as was shown by the extraordinary scenes at Berlin in 1920 during the shooting of a film which gave in a new mass medium a biography of the greatest of Prussia's rulers. Serious historical works, polemical studies and impressionistic journalism helped to keep his memory green.

Between the wars the most influential historians of Frederick were Frederick Meinecke and Gerhard Ritter. Meinecke thought the key to an understanding of Frederick lay in the dichotomy between the enlightened ideas which moulded his character and intellect and the idea of political necessity which guided his acts. Ritter on the other hand was mainly concerned to make clear what Frederick had actually achieved in the historical circumstances of his own time, and how these achievements had affected history. After the downfall of the Third *Reich*, he asserted that he had also delicately implied a comparison between Frederick and Hitler. Whereas Frederick had limited objectives in foreign policy Hitler's ambitions were limitless. While the Frederician state had been based on religious toleration and voluntary limitation of state activity to external things, Hitler had avowed his determination to mould the German people by force and propaganda into conformity with the Nazi ideal. While as a frontline soldier in the First World War Ritter had felt

that Frederick was fighting by his side, he quoted
against the Nazi conception of the state Kant's
saying that the state is concerned with law and
not at all with morals. Fortunately for himself the
comparison was so delicately drawn that it
escaped notice at the time and was only made
explicit after the Second World War in a new
edition of Ritter's biography.

Hitler himself had no doubts about the legiti-
macy and paternity of the Third *Reich*, which was
proclaimed in the garrison church at Potsdam in
the vault where lay the coffins of Frederick the
Great and his father Frederick William I. Immediately after President Hindenburg had proclaimed the new empire, Chancellor Hitler placed
a crown of laurel leaves, worked in gold, on
Frederick's coffin. Though Frederick had been
dead for a century and a half, political miracles
were still being worked at his shrine.

While Hindenburg's political role in post-war
Germany was largely based on the idea that he
personified Hohenzollern traditions and Hitler's
success was at least partly due to his misrepresen-
tation of his régime as the lineal and legitimate
successor of Hohenzollern absolutism, they had
no monopoly in appealing to Frederick the Great.
In 1936, while still in the service of Hitler's
government, Carl Goerdeler prepared a state paper
in which he claimed that 'salvation for Germany
and for the world could be obtained only by self-

control, by pursuing modest goals, and by prac-
tising strict economy after the manner of Frederick
the Great'.[1] The rejection of such ideas by both
Hitler and Goering on the ground that they would
mean postponement if not reduction of their plans
for rearmament cost Goerdeler their confidence
and ultimately led to his becoming the acknowledged leader of underground resistance.

Hitler's defeat convinced German historians
that at some point or other Germany must have
taken the wrong turning. When something has
failed, or even seems for a time to have failed, historians are never at a loss to explain why it failed.
In the vigorous debate which is still going on in
Germany various turning points have been suggested at which Prussia may be said to have
deviated with disastrous results from her old ideals
and traditions. Although Dehio has suggested that
his countrymen might place their memories of
Frederick the Great and Bismarck in a display
cabinet, as they do the costly silver which they no
longer use on their dinner tables, few German historians seem to have looked as far back as the
reign of Frederick the Great for this turning point.

There is still a tendency to identify Frederick as
the supreme representative of genuine Prussian
ideals and to judge later régimes by his basic ideas
on state and society. This is to deny or at least

[1] G. Ritter, *The German Resistance* (translated by R. T. Clark,
London, 1958), p. 34.

ignore that the essence of the Prussian system of government, as developed by Frederick the Great, was the refusal to give the chance of a political education to the middle and lower classes. Frederick's success tended to perpetuate and fossilize an administrative and social system which steadily lost touch with the political realities of nineteenth- and twentieth-century Europe. Yet this system contrived to extend its influence over the rest of Germany, to draw Germany away from contact with west European liberalism and to make her the associate and bulwark of the east European despotic empires ruled by the Hapsburgs and the Romanovs. Lack of political experience contributed to the failure of German liberalism in 1848 and left the way clear for Bismarck who, alike in his denial of political education to the mass of the German people and his uncompromising opposition to responsible government, was Frederick's true, and fatal, heir.

Even after the collapse of the Hohenzollern *Reich* and the emergence of the Weimar Republic, Hitler, though not himself a Prussian, thought it worth while to invoke the historical myth of Frederick the Great and to represent or rather misrepresent himself as the standard bearer of Prussian traditions. Once again, as at Frankfurt in 1848, Germany failed to achieve representative and responsible government with the same fatal consequences for herself and for Europe.

Bibliography

BOOKS IN ENGLISH FOR FURTHER READING

LIVES OF FREDERICK. Thomas Carlyle's pioneer *History of Frederick II of Prussia* (various editions) heads the list. W. F. Reddaway, *Frederick the Great and the Rise of Prussia* (New York 1904), though almost as dated as Carlyle, is still worth reading. There is an English translation by R. A. Bell of Pierre Gaxotte, *Frederick the Great* (London 1941). G. P. Gooch's *Frederick the Great* (London 1947) unfortunately consists of detached essays on aspects of Frederick's career. Edith Simon, *The Making of Frederick the Great* (London 1963), offers a lively and readable account of Frederick's career up to 1745 and is to be followed by a second volume on his later life.

THE RISE OF PRUSSIA. W. H. Bruford's chapter on 'The Organization and Rise of Prussia' in volume 7 of the *New Cambridge Modern History* gives a valuable conspectus. In some ways C. T. Atkinson, *A History of Germany* (London 1908) still offers the best short treatment of the military and political rise of Prussia under Frederick II. W. L. Dorn's three articles in the *Political Science Quarterly* vols. 46 and 47 are indispensable on the Prussian bureaucracy under Frederick, while R. A. Dorwart, *The Administrative Reforms of Frederick William I of Prussia* (Cambridge, Mass. 1953) gives a good description of the administrative system which Frederick inherited and, in essence, maintained. Hans Rosenberg, *Bureaucracy, Aristocracy and Autocracy. The Prussian Experience 1660–1815* (Harvard U.P. 1958) offers a sociological study of the Prussian Civil Service 'as an authoritarian political group'.

FREDERICK'S DIPLOMACY AND WARS. The *New Cambridge Modern History* VII has chapters on the War of the Austrian Succession, the Diplomatic Revolution and the Seven Years War, which place these successive episodes in Frederick's career in their European setting. In view of the author's special interest in Prussian history, W. L. Dorn, *Competition for Empire* (New York 1940)—a general survey of European history from 1740 to 1763—is particularly useful on Frederick the Great's career. Sir Richard Lodge in his *Great Britain and Prussia in the Eighteenth Century* (Oxford 1923) sketched the diplomatic relations of these two states in the reign of Frederick II. His *Studies in Eighteenth Century Diplomacy* (London 1930) review in detail the diplomacy of the Austrian Succession War which marked Prussia's rise to greatness. For Frederick's attitude to and responsibility for the first partition of Poland, see Herbert H. Kaplan, *The First Partition of Poland* (Columbia University Press 1962). There is little else on Frederick's external policies after 1763 except H. Temperley, *Frederick the Great and Kaiser Joseph* (London 1915). W. O. Henderson, *Studies in the Economic Policy of Frederick the Great* (Frank Cass and Co. Ltd. 1963) is useful on the economic side.

RECOMMENDED READING IN FRENCH AND GERMAN

Students who can read German are advised to begin further reading on Frederick the Great with Gerhard Ritter, *Friedrich der Grosse ein historisches Profil* (3rd edition, Heidelberg 1954). Anyone interested in Frederick, who can read French, would gain by dipping into the collected edition of his works, *Oeuvres de Frédéric le Grand* (30 vols. Berlin 1846–57). There is a convenient edition of the three major historical works in which Frederick recorded the events of his reign down to 1778, edited by E. Boutaric and E. Campardon in 2 vols. (Paris 1866). The basic primary source for the politics of his reign is the classic edition of his own *Politische Correspondenz* 46 vols. (Berlin 1879–1939). The contemporary British attitude to Frederick and Prussia is the theme of Manfred Schlenke, *England und das friderianizische Preussen 1740-1763* (Verlag Karl Alber, 1963.)

THE RISE OF PRUSSIA. The best general survey of Prussian history is still probably Otto Hintze, *Die Hohenzollern und ihr Werk* (2nd edition, Berlin 1915), while the best general text book on the internal development of Prussia is F. Hartung, *Deutsche Verfassungsgeschichte vom 15 Jahrhundert bis zum Gegenwart* (6th edition, Stuttgart 1954). Max Braubach deals admirably with the reign of Frederick II in *Handbuch der deutschen Geschichte* (new edition, ed. Grundmann Vol. II Stuttgart 1955) and supplies a useful list of books for further reading.

IMPORTANT DATES

	in FREDERICK'S LIFE	in THE RISE OF PRUSSIA
1701		Elector Frederick III becomes first king in Prussia.
1702–13		Prussia takes part in war of the Spanish Succession.
1712	Born on 24 January.	
1713		Prussia gains Spanish Gelderland. Accession of Frederick William I.
1720		Prussia acquires Stettin and part of Pomerania at the end of the Second Northern War.
1730	Attempts to escape abroad. Imprisoned at Küstrin.	
1732	Removes to Neu-Ruppin.	
1733	Married on 12 June.	
1734	Serves under Prince Eugene on the Rhine.	
1736	Establishes himself at Rheinsberg.	
1739	Writes the *Anti-Machiavel*.	
1740	Succeeds to the throne on 31 May. Takes the title King of the Prussians.	Death of Frederick William I.
1741	Makes an alliance with France.	Battle of Mollwitz, first victory of Prussians over Austrians.
1742	Concludes the convention of Klein-Schnellendorf.	Acquisition of Silesia and Glatz by the treaty of Berlin. Acquisition of East Friesland with Emden.
1744	Wins the battle of Chotusitz.	Treaty of Dresden confirms acquisition of Silesia and Glatz.
1745	Wins battles at Hohenfriedberg and Soor.	
1745–7	Builds the palace of Sans Souci.	
1745–55		Legal reforms of Cocceji.
1748		Treaty of Aix-la-Chapelle guarantees Silesia and Glatz to Prussia.

1750–3	Entertains Voltaire.	
1755	Signs the convention of Westminster with Britain.	Breakdown of Austro–British alliance. Austria and France conclude first treaty of Versailles.
1756	Invades Saxony on 29 August.	Beginning of Continental Seven Years War. European coalition formed against Prussia.
1757	Fails to conquer Bohemia (May–June). Wins victories at Rossbach and Leuthen (Nov.–Dec.).	
1758	Beats the Russians at Zorndorf.	Britain subsidizes Prussia. Britain saves western Germany from France at Minden.
1759	Beaten by the Russians at Kunersdorf.	
1760	Wins victories at Liegnitz and Torgau.	
1762	Quarrels with Bute. Concludes an alliance with Peter III. Makes peace with Austria.	Death of Tsaritsa Elizabeth on 5 January. Deposition of Peter III on 9 July.
1763		Treaty of Hubertusburg finally secures Silesia for Prussia.
1764	Allies himself with Catherine II.	Russia and Prussia place Poniatowski on the Polish throne.
1766	Sets up the *Régie*.	Prince Henry visits Catherine II.
1769–70	Meets Joseph II at Neisse and Neustadt.	
1770–1		
1772–5		Prussia gains West Prussia and is recognized as an equal partner in the First Partition of Poland.
1778	Fights his last campaign.	Treaty of Teschen thwarts Austrian aggression in Germany.
1779		
1780–1	Loses the Russian alliance.	
1785	Founds the League of German princes.	Joseph II abandons Bavarian exchange project. Accession of Frederick William II. Triple Alliance of Britain, Prussia and the United Provinces.
1786	Dies on 17 August.	
1788		
1791		Anspach and Bayreuth annexed to Prussia.
1795		Prussian legal code promulgated.

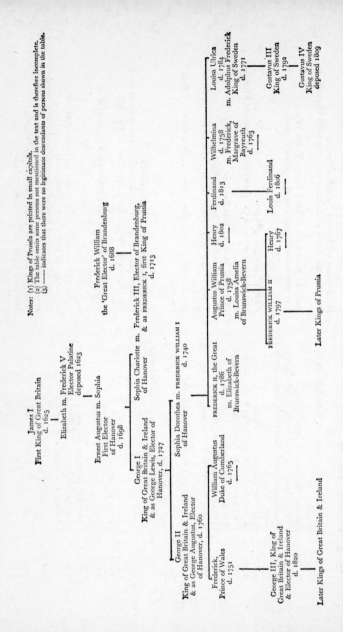

Notes: (1) Kings of Prussia are printed in small capitals.
(2) The table omits some persons not mentioned in the text and is therefore incomplete.
(3) ——— indicates that there were no legitimate descendants of persons shown in the table.

James I
First King of Great Britain
d. 1625

Elizabeth m. Frederick V
Elector Palatine
deposed 1623

Ernest Augustus m. Sophia
First Elector
of Hanover
d. 1698

Frederick William
the 'Great Elector' of Brandenburg
d. 1688

Sophia Charlotte m. Frederick III, Elector of Brandenburg,
& as FREDERICK I, first King of Prussia
of Hanover   d. 1713

George I
King of Great Britain & Ireland
& as George Lewis, Elector of
Hanover, d. 1727

Sophia Dorothea m. FREDERICK WILLIAM I
of Hanover   d. 1740

George II
King of Great Britain & Ireland
& as George Augustus, Elector
of Hanover, d. 1760

FREDERICK II, the Great
d. 1786
m. Elizabeth of
Brunswick-Bevern

Augustus William
Prince of Prussia
d. 1758
m. Louisa Amelia
of Brunswick-Bevern

Henry
d. 1802

Ferdinand
d. 1813

Wilhelmina
d. 1758
m. Frederick,
Margrave of
Bayreuth
d. 1763

Louisa Ulrica
d. 1784
m. Adolphus Frederick
King of Sweden
d. 1771

William Augustus
Duke of Cumberland
d. 1765

Henry
d. 1767

Louis Ferdinand
d. 1806

Gustavus III
King of Sweden
d. 1792

Frederick,
Prince of Wales
d. 1751

FREDERICK WILLIAM II
d. 1797

Gustavus IV
King of Sweden
deposed 1809

George III, King of
Great Britain & Ireland
& Elector of Hanover
d. 1820

Later Kings of Prussia

Later Kings of Great Britain & Ireland

Index